Higher
Modern Studies

2006 Exam
Paper 1
Paper 2 Decision Making Exercise 1
Paper 2 Decision Making Exercise 2

2007 SQP
Paper 1
Paper 2 Decision Making Exercise

2007 Exam
Paper 1
Paper 2 Decision Making Exercise

2008 Exam
Paper 1
Paper 2 Decision Making Exercise

Leckie×Leckie

First exam published in 2006.

Published by Leckie & Leckie Ltd, 3rd Floor, 4 Queen Street, Edinburgh EH2 1JE

tel: 0131 220 6831 fax: 0131 225 9987 enquiries@leckieandleckie.co.uk www.leckieandleckie.co.uk

ISBN 978-1-84372-684-5

A CIP Catalogue record for this book is available from the British Library.

Leckie & Leckie is a division of Huveaux plc.

Leckie & Leckie is grateful to the copyright holders, as credited at the back of the book, for permission to use their material.

Every effort has been made to trace the copyright holders and to obtain their permission for the use of copyright material.

Leckie & Leckie will gladly receive information enabling them to rectify any error or omission in subsequent editions.

[BLANK PAGE]

X064/301

NATIONAL
QUALIFICATIONS
2006

MONDAY, 15 MAY
9.00 AM – 10.25 AM

MODERN STUDIES

HIGHER

Paper 1

Candidates should answer **three** questions –

One from Section A: *Political Issues in the United Kingdom*. Each question is worth 20 marks.

One from Section B: *Social Issues in the United Kingdom*. Each question is worth 10 marks.

One from Section C: *International Issues*. Each question is worth 20 marks.

Marks may be deducted for bad spelling and bad punctuation and for writing that is difficult to read.

SCOTTISH
QUALIFICATIONS
AUTHORITY
©

SECTION A—Political Issues in the United Kingdom
Answer ONE question from this Section
Each question is worth 20 marks

Marks

STUDY THEME 1: DECISION MAKING IN CENTRAL GOVERNMENT

Question A1

(*a*) Describe the powers and responsibilities of the Prime Minister. **10**

(*b*) To what extent do the media influence decision-making in central government? **10**
(20)

STUDY THEME 2: THE GOVERNMENT OF SCOTLAND

Question A2

(*a*) Describe the powers and responsibilities of Scottish local authorities. **10**

(*b*) To what extent has devolution changed the way in which decisions are made for Scotland? **10**
(20)

STUDY THEME 3: POLITICAL PARTIES AND THEIR POLICIES

Question A3

(*a*) Describe the organisation of **one** of the following political parties:

Conservative;

Labour;

Liberal Democrat. **10**

(*b*) Examine the success of the Scottish National Party in recent elections. **10**
(20)

*STUDY THEME 4: THE ELECTORAL SYSTEM, VOTING AND
POLITICAL ATTITUDES*

Question A4

(*a*) Other than the media, what factors influence voting behaviour? **10**

(*b*) *There are fairer electoral systems than First Past The Post.*
Discuss. **10**
(20)

SECTION B — Social Issues in the United Kingdom

Answer ONE question from this Section

Each question is worth 10 marks

Marks

STUDY THEME 5: INCOME AND WEALTH IN THE UNITED KINGDOM

Question B5

(*a*)   In what ways can social class be defined?   **(10)**

OR

(*b*)   What evidence is there that **either** women **or** ethnic minorities experience discrimination?   **(10)**

OR

(*c*)   What criticisms have been made of the Government's welfare to work policies?   **(10)**

STUDY THEME 6: HEALTH CARE IN THE UNITED KINGDOM

Question B6

(*a*)   Describe the ways in which government encourages individuals to take responsibility for their health.   **(10)**

OR

(*b*)   What evidence is there of health inequalities in the UK?   **(10)**

OR

(*c*)   What criticisms have been made of the provision of primary health care?   **(10)**

[Turn over

SECTION C — International Issues

Answer ONE question from this Section

Each question is worth 20 marks

Marks

STUDY THEME 7: A SOCIETY IN CHANGE — SOUTH AFRICA

Question C7

(a) Describe the main features of the political system in South Africa. **10**

(b) To what extent has the South African Government been successful in dealing with **two** of the following issues:

education;

housing;

land ownership? **10**

(20)

STUDY THEME 8: A SOCIETY IN CHANGE — CHINA

Question C8

(a) In what ways have China's people benefited from recent economic reforms? **10**

(b) *The Communist Party may encourage social reform, but continues to discourage any political reform.*

Discuss. **10**

(20)

STUDY THEME 9: ETHNIC MINORITIES IN THE USA

Question C9

(a) What evidence is there that the American Dream has been achieved by members of ethnic minority groups? **10**

(b) *Immigration is an issue over which public opinion in the USA is divided.*

Discuss. **10**

(20)

Marks

STUDY THEME 10: THE EUROPEAN UNION

Question C10

(a) Describe the powers and responsibilities of **two** of the following European Union institutions:

the Commission;

the Council of Ministers;

the Parliament. **10**

(b) Examine the social and economic benefits of enlargement. **10**

(20)

STUDY THEME 11: GLOBAL SECURITY

Question C11

(a) Describe the achievements of the North Atlantic Treaty Organisation (NATO). **10**

(b) *Concerns about the ways in which the United Nations (UN) deals with threats to global security have led to proposals for its reform.*

Discuss. **10**

(20)

STUDY THEME 12: THE POLITICS OF FOOD

Question C12

With reference to specific countries in Africa (excluding the Republic of South Africa) answer the questions below.

(a) Describe the work of Non-Governmental Organisations (NGOs) in the production and distribution of food. **10**

(b) *Government actions are the main cause of food insecurity.*

Discuss. **10**

(20)

[END OF QUESTION PAPER]

[BLANK PAGE]

X064/302

NATIONAL
QUALIFICATIONS
2006

MONDAY, 15 MAY
10.45 AM – 12.05 PM

MODERN STUDIES
HIGHER
Paper 2
Decision Making Exercise 1

Attempt

Either   Decision Making Exercise 1: Income and Wealth in the United Kingdom;

Or   Decision Making Exercise 2: Health Care in the United Kingdom but **not both**.
The Decision Making Exercises are contained in separate booklets.

A summary of the exercise is provided on the cover of each booklet.

Read the summaries carefully before deciding which exercise to attempt. In each case, answer **all** questions.

DECISION MAKING EXERCISE 1

INCOME AND WEALTH IN THE UNITED KINGDOM

Summary of Decision Making Exercise

You are an adviser to the Department of Work and Pensions (DWP). You have been asked to prepare a report in which you recommend or reject the proposal that the Government abolish the right of UK employers to set compulsory retirement ages.

Before beginning the task, you must answer a number of short evaluating questions (Questions 1-3) based on the source material provided. The source material is as follows:

    SOURCE A: Facing Up To The Demographic Time Bomb

    SOURCE B: Keep Compulsory Retirement Ages

    SOURCE C: Statistical Information

SCOTTISH
QUALIFICATIONS
AUTHORITY

©

SOURCE A: FACING UP TO THE DEMOGRAPHIC TIME BOMB

The UK faces a demographic time bomb. The share of the population taken up by each age group in the over sixty-fives is set to keep on increasing for the foreseeable future. At the same time, the birth rate is falling. It does not take a genius to work out that the figures do not add up. The prospect of a greatly increased retired population being
5   dependent on a reduced workforce is upon us. This is a problem that demands a solution – now!

People over 65 are actually legally entitled to work. However, it is difficult for them to find companies willing to take them on or keep them in employment. This is because most companies enforce a compulsory retirement age of 65. Yet there are powerful
10   reasons why people should be allowed to work beyond the age of 65. For some people it is a financial disaster for them to retire when they are required to. A variety of factors have made it difficult, if not impossible, for them to save for their future. Work is a social experience and being forced to retire before one feels ready to can be a traumatic experience. The world has moved on since the setting up of the welfare state. Today's
15   65 year olds are very different from those of the 1940s. The 65 year olds of the future will differ even more so. Already, an overwhelming majority of the over-50s intend to remain in paid employment well past any retirement date.

Scrapping retirement ages does not mean that people should remain in paid employment regardless of fitness or competence. Employers already use trade union
20   approved methods to monitor and evaluate the performance of staff. However, it would mean a change to the circumstances in which long service employees ended their working days. Instead of being "pensioned off", they could now retire with dignity. With government placing such a large emphasis on the importance of giving choice in other areas of social policy, it is surely time to extend it to employment. Everyone
25   wins – employers, employees and even the Treasury in relation to both tax revenues and benefit spending. Abolishing compulsory retirement ages is clearly the right thing to do.

David McQueen, Age Concern Spokesperson

SOURCE B: **KEEP COMPULSORY RETIREMENT AGES**

Recent proposals to abolish the compulsory retirement ages set by employers must be resisted. This is a misguided approach to solving what is rightly recognised as a demographic challenge but whose effects have been somewhat overstated. In relation to both our European and non-European competitors, our state benefits take up a smaller

5   share of our Gross Domestic Product (GDP). There is no evidence to suggest that this is likely to change in the future.

The fact of the matter is that older people have always been more costly to employ than younger ones. Companies have tended to pay younger workers less than their productivity justifies, and older workers more, to persuade the young to stay on and

10   move up the pay scale. Yet employers have always been flexible in their employment practices with key workers being given the option to work on beyond a certain age. Most companies also have policies in place to deal with ageist attitudes in the workplace. However, a formal retirement age is one of the few ways a company can maintain a balanced, dynamic workforce. Abolish it and employers will be faced with the prospect

15   of having to retain older workers whose health and productivity are poor. The costs to industry in terms of health benefits, sickness and death-in-service benefits will be huge.

Of course, there will always be those who wish to keep on in employment until they are forced to stop. However, many people look forward to retirement. Admittedly, some may be financially unprepared for retirement, but this has had less to do with

20   demography and more to do with gaps in their employment record. Whereas the efforts of social inclusion policies to keep such gaps to a minimum are to be applauded, it would be wrong to give workers the flexibility to retire when they want to. Scrap compulsory retirement ages and the circumstances in which long-serving employees end their working days would certainly change. They would leave with the sack instead of a

25   presentation and goodwill. The end point of the employer-employee relationship must be defined. Otherwise we lose our competitive edge, our prosperity suffers and everyone loses out.

Lisa Newman , CBI Spokesperson

[Turn over for Source C on *Pages four* and *five*

SOURCE C: STATISTICAL INFORMATION

SOURCE C1: Actual and projected percentages of selected age groups in the UK population, 1946 – 2041.

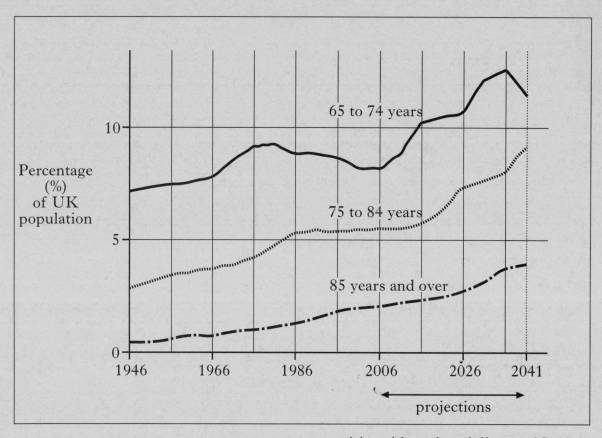

Adapted from *Annual Abstract of Statistics*

SOURCE C2: Spending on state benefits in selected countries as a percentage of GDP.

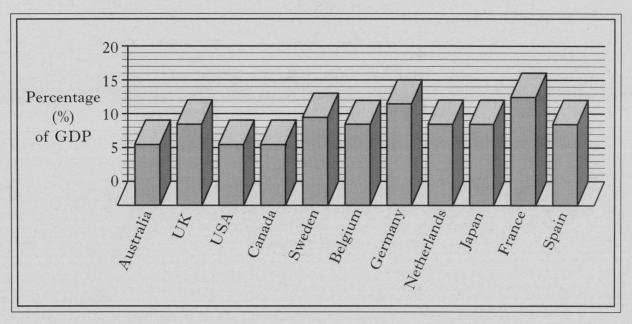

Adapted from *The Economist*, 2004

SOURCE C3: Workforce profile

- At the moment there are 1·1 non workers for every worker
- By 2031, there will be three non-workers for every worker
- 50% of over-50s plan to stay in work beyond retirement date
- 23% of over-50s say they will work until forced to stop
- 80% of over-50s say they have experienced ageist rejection when applying for jobs

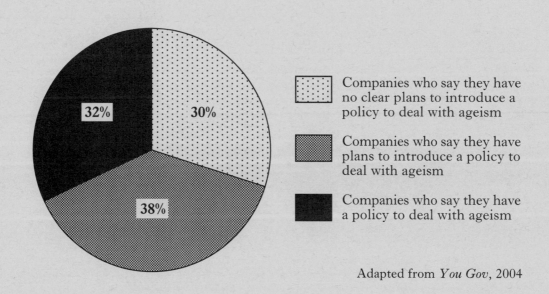

Adapted from *You Gov*, 2004

[BLANK PAGE]

DECISION MAKING EXERCISE 1

QUESTIONS

Marks

Questions 1 to 3 are based on Sources A to C on pages 2–5. Answer Questions 1 to 3 before attempting Question 4.

In Questions 1 to 3, use only the Sources described in each question.

Question 1

(a) Use **only** *Source C1 and Source A*.

To what extent does the evidence support David McQueen?   **2**

(b) Use **only** *Source C2 and Source B*.

To what extent does the evidence support Lisa Newman?   **2**

Question 2

(a) Use **only** *Source C3 and Source A*.

Why might David McQueen be accused of exaggeration?   **2**

(b) Use **only** *Source C3 and Source B*.

Why might Lisa Newman be accused of exaggeration?   **2**

Question 3

Use **only** *Source A* and *Source B*.

Contrast the views of David McQueen and Lisa Newman on the circumstances in which people would end their working days if compulsory retirement ages were abolished.   **2**

(10)

Question 4   *Marks*

DECISION MAKING TASK

You are an adviser to the Department of Work and Pensions (DWP). You have been asked to prepare a report in which you recommend or reject the proposal that the Government abolish the right of UK employers to set compulsory retirement ages.

In your report you should:

*   recommend or reject the proposal to abolish the right of UK employers to set compulsory retirement ages;

*   provide arguments to support your recommendation;

*   identify and comment on any arguments which may be presented by those who oppose your recommendation.

In your report you **must** use:

*   the **source material** provided and

*   other **background knowledge**.

Your answer should be written in a style appropriate to a *report*.

The written and statistical sources which have been provided are as follows:

SOURCE A: Facing Up To The Demographic Time Bomb

SOURCE B: Keep Compulsory Retirement Ages

SOURCE C: Statistical Information   **(20)**

Total: 30 Marks

[END OF QUESTION PAPER]

X064/303

NATIONAL
QUALIFICATIONS
2006

MONDAY, 15 MAY
10.45 AM – 12.05 PM

MODERN STUDIES
HIGHER
Paper 2
Decision Making Exercise 2

Attempt

Either   Decision Making Exercise 1: Income and Wealth in the United Kingdom;

Or   Decision Making Exercise 2: Health Care in the United Kingdom but **not both**.
The Decision Making Exercises are contained in separate booklets.

A summary of the exercise is provided on the cover of each booklet.

Read the summaries carefully before deciding which exercise to attempt. In each case, answer **all** questions.

DECISION MAKING EXERCISE 2

HEALTH CARE IN THE UNITED KINGDOM

Summary of Decision Making Exercise

You are a health policy expert. You have been asked to prepare a report for a health care pressure group in which you recommend or reject the proposal to involve privately run treatment centres in the Scottish NHS.

Before beginning the task, you must answer a number of short evaluating questions (Questions 1-3) based on the source material provided. The source material is as follows:

SOURCE A: The Best Treatment For Waiting Lists

SOURCE B: The NHS Deserves Better Treatment

SOURCE C: Statistical Information

SCOTTISH
QUALIFICATIONS
AUTHORITY

SOURCE A: NEWSPAPER EDITORIAL: THE BEST TREATMENT FOR WAITING LISTS

Since their involvement in the English NHS in 2004, privately run treatment centres have had a huge effect on waiting lists with an extra 250 000 operations being performed each year. All of these operations have been performed on the NHS, free at the point of use, and much sooner than would otherwise have been possible. Treatment centres
5   specialise in the provision of operations like eye cataracts, hip and knee replacements and other routine surgery procedures. They are not part of a general hospital. They do not have to deal with life-threatening emergency operations. Consequently they never need to cancel booked appointments, and resources are used more efficiently.

The use made of these centres by the NHS is another beneficial example of
10   co-operation between the NHS and the private sector. Contracts to run some of these treatment centres have been given to private companies from Canada, South Africa and the USA. They have been promised some government funding for their first five years to help cover their start up costs. These companies can bring their own teams of highly qualified doctors and surgeons with them. However, they are allowed to recruit up to
15   seventy per cent of their workforce from the NHS, as long as no local primary care trusts (PCTs) have any objections. As a result of this co-operation, NHS trusts in England have another option when a combination of high demand and staff shortages leads to lengthy waiting lists. They can now choose to have their operations done by a privately run treatment centre. Each operation performed in a treatment centre is paid
20   for, at no extra cost, from taxation. The treatments are also far cheaper than they would be if purchased from private hospitals in the United Kingdom.

The performance of the NHS south of the border continues to improve. In recent years, waiting lists in England have been halved. One of the main reasons for this reduction has been the use of privately run treatment centres. In Scotland, until
25   recently, there has been no such option. Despite spending more per person on health care than its English counterpart, the Scottish NHS has achieved none of its waiting time targets. The involvement of privately run treatment centres in the Scottish NHS will surely allow it to perform more efficiently.

The Editor

**SOURCE B: LETTER TO THE EDITOR: THE NHS DESERVES BETTER
                TREATMENT**

In return for their involvement in the English NHS, privately run treatment centres
have been guaranteed a fixed number of patients over a five-year period. The aim of
this agreement is to reduce waiting lists. However, the overall effects on these have been
slight. Of the 250 000 "extra" annual operations performed by these treatment centres,
5   115 000 could, and should, have been carried out in NHS hospitals. To enable
treatment centres to receive their guaranteed quota of patients, work has been
transferred from NHS trusts. As a result of this, some departments in English NHS
hospitals have lost more than half of their total case load.

Any loss of patients affects staff numbers, training opportunities and a hospital's ability
10 to offer a full range of services. Less surgery means less funding. Junior doctors do not
get the opportunity to witness, let alone perform, routine operations. With so much of
their work being transferred, local trusts have no real choice other than to allow their
staff to leave. And where do they find employment? That's right – in the private sector.
These privately run treatment centres have been forced on unwilling local NHS
15 organisations and are nothing more than a step closer to the complete privatisation of
health care. In some areas where these centres are being used, it is not because of staff
shortages at all, but lack of beds. Here in Scotland, there has been no rise in emergency
admissions and, in any case, the Scottish NHS is better off for beds than the English
NHS.

20 Privately run treatment centres mean greater inequality in health care. Private providers
are always going to treat the most profitable cases. Local trusts will be left to deal with
the most difficult ones. Those who recommend the use of treatment centres point to the
advantages of "choice". Any patient who has been on a hospital waiting list for more
than six months may choose to be referred to one for treatment. However, people totally
25 reject the notion that having more choice over where they are treated is important. By
draining funding from essential services, treatment centres have had a very damaging
effect on health care efficiency. What the NHS in Scotland needs is the right
management and public investment. It can do without money being thrown at privately
run treatment centres.

Euan Ross

[Turn over for Source C on *Pages four* and *five*

SOURCE C: STATISTICAL INFORMATION

SOURCE C1:   (a)   NHS spending per head in the UK, 1998–2003

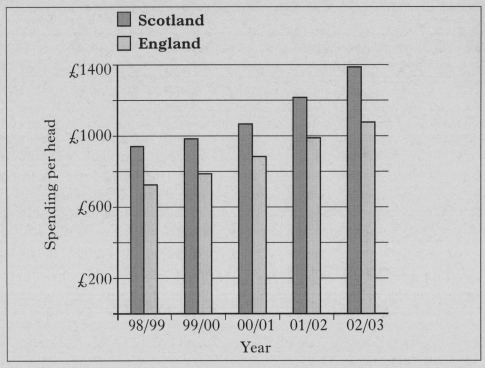

Adapted from *The Herald*, 2004

SOURCE C1:   (b)   Waiting time targets report (Scotland)

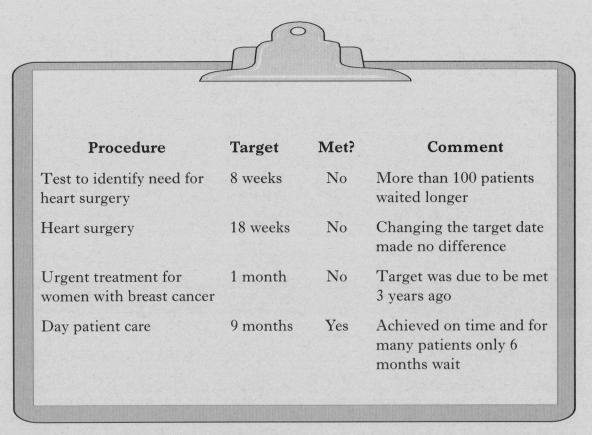

Procedure	Target	Met?	Comment
Test to identify need for heart surgery	8 weeks	No	More than 100 patients waited longer
Heart surgery	18 weeks	No	Changing the target date made no difference
Urgent treatment for women with breast cancer	1 month	No	Target was due to be met 3 years ago
Day patient care	9 months	Yes	Achieved on time and for many patients only 6 months wait

Adapted from *The Herald*, 2004

SOURCE C2:

(a) Emergency admissions to hospital in Scotland, (selected age groups), 1981–2002

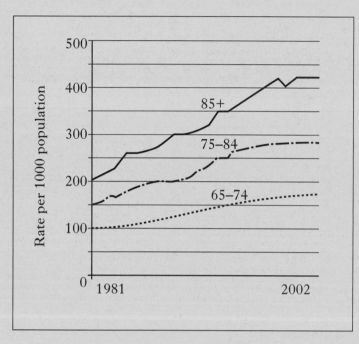

Adapted from *The Herald*, 2004

(b) NHS bed provision in the UK

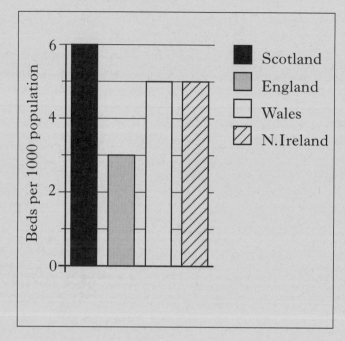

Adapted from *The Herald*, 2004

SOURCE C3: Public opinion survey

How important is it to you to have more choice over which hospital treats you?

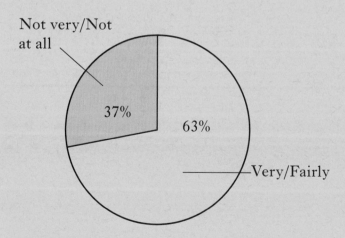

Adapted from *The Economist*, 2004

[BLANK PAGE]

DECISION MAKING EXERCISE 2

QUESTIONS

Marks

Questions 1 to 3 are based on Sources A to C on pages 2–5. Answer Questions 1 to 3 before attempting Question 4.

In Questions 1 to 3, use <u>only</u> the Sources described in each question.

Question 1

Use **only** *Source A and Source B.*

Contrast the views of the Editor and Euan Ross on the effects of treatment centres on waiting lists.

2

Question 2

(*a*) *Use* **only** *Source C1(a), C1(b) and Source A.*

To what extent does the evidence support the Editor?

3

(*b*) *Use* **only** *Source C2(a), C2(b) and Source B.*

To what extent does the evidence support Euan Ross?

3

Question 3

Use **only** *Source C3 and Source B.*

Why might Euan Ross be accused of exaggeration?

2

(10)

Question 4

Marks

DECISION MAKING TASK

You are a health policy expert. You have been asked to prepare a report for a health care pressure group in which you recommend or reject the proposal to involve privately run treatment centres in the Scottish NHS.

In your report you should:

* recommend or reject the proposed involvement of privately run treatment centres in the Scottish NHS;

* provide arguments to support your recommendation;

* identify and comment on any arguments which may be presented by those who oppose your recommendation.

In your report you **must** use:

* the **source material** provided and

* other **background knowledge**.

Your answer should be written in a style appropriate to a *report*.

The written and statistical sources which have been provided are as follows:

SOURCE A: The Best Treatment For Waiting Lists

SOURCE B: The NHS Deserves Better Treatment

SOURCE C: Statistical Information

(20)

Total: 30 Marks

[END OF QUESTION PAPER]

In Paper 1, there is one 15 mark essay on each Study Theme, as opposed to 10 mark descriptive or analytical items.

Paper 1 is now worth 60 marks as opposed to 50 under the old examination.

There is now only one Decision Making Exercise contained in Paper 2. Some of the Study Themes have been re-titled to reflect changes in content.

[BLANK PAGE]

ModStds/SQP285

Modern Studies	Time: 1 hour 30 mins	NATIONAL

Higher   QUALIFICATIONS

Paper 1

Specimen Question Paper

for use in and after 2007

Candidates should answer **FOUR** questions:

ONE from Section A

and

ONE from Section B

and

ONE from Section C

and

ONE OTHER from **EITHER** Section A **OR** Section C

Each question is worth 15 marks.

Section A: Political Issues in the United Kingdom.

Section B: Social Issues in the United Kingdom.

Section C: International Issues.

SCOTTISH
QUALIFICATIONS
AUTHORITY

SECTION A—Political Issues in the United Kingdom
Each question is worth 15 marks

STUDY THEME 1A: DEVOLVED DECISION MAKING IN SCOTLAND

Question A1

To what extent are the functions of local authorities limited by the Scottish and United Kingdom Parliaments?

STUDY THEME 1B: DECISION MAKING IN CENTRAL GOVERNMENT

Question A2

Critically examine the view that pressure groups are a threat to democracy.

STUDY THEME 1C: POLITICAL PARTIES AND THEIR POLICIES (INCLUDING THE SCOTTISH DIMENSION)

Question A3

With reference to at least two political parties:

To what extent do their policies on **two** of the following differ?

          Education   Law and Order   Taxation

STUDY THEME 1D: ELECTORAL SYSTEMS, VOTING AND POLITICAL ATTITUDES

Question A4

Some factors are more important than others in influencing voting behaviour.

Discuss.

SECTION B — Social Issues in the United Kingdom

Each question is worth 15 marks

STUDY THEME 2: WEALTH AND HEALTH INEQUALITIES IN THE UNITED KINGDOM

Question B5

To what extent is there a link between income and health?

Question B6

Critically examine the success of recent government measures to reduce gender inequalities.

SECTION C — International Issues
Each question is worth 15 marks

STUDY THEME 3A: THE REPUBLIC OF SOUTH AFRICA

Question C7

To what extent do different groups live separate and unequal lives?

STUDY THEME 3B: THE PEOPLE'S REPUBLIC OF CHINA

Question C8

There is little demand for political reform because of recent gains from economic and social reform.

Discuss.

STUDY THEME 3C: THE UNITED STATES OF AMERICA

Question C9

Assess the effectiveness of government policies to reduce economic and social inequalities.

STUDY THEME 3D: THE EUROPEAN UNION

Question C10

Assess the effectiveness of the European Parliament in EU decision making.

STUDY THEME 3E: THE POLITICS OF DEVELOPMENT IN AFRICA

Question C11

With reference to specific African countries (excluding the Republic of South Africa):

Government domestic policies have been the main obstacles to economic and social development.

Discuss.

STUDY THEME 3F: GLOBAL SECURITY

Question C12

To what extent have there been changes in both the role and membership of NATO?

[END OF SPECIMEN QUESTION PAPER]

ModStds/SQP285

Modern Studies	Time: 1 hour 15 mins	NATIONAL
Higher		QUALIFICATIONS
Paper 2		
Decision Making Exercise		

Specimen Question Paper
for use in and after 2007

Summary of Decision Making Exercise

You are a leading academic in the field of social policy. You have been asked to prepare a report for the Scottish Executive in which you recommend or reject the proposal to introduce means testing for the provision of personal care for elderly people in Scotland.

Before beginning the task, you must answer a number of evaluating questions (Questions 1–3) based on the source material provided. The source material is:

SOURCE A: Caring for the Elderly

SOURCE B1:   Say "No" to Means Testing Personal Care!

SOURCE B2:   Say "Yes" to Means Testing Personal Care!

SOURCE C: Statistical Information

SCOTTISH
QUALIFICATIONS
AUTHORITY

SOURCE A: CARING FOR THE ELDERLY

Providing care for our elderly is one of the biggest challenges facing today's politicians. The percentage of elderly people in the UK population is projected to grow while that of working age will decline significantly. This has serious consequences for the Welfare State.

5   Social Security is the largest item of Government spending, followed by health care. NHS treatment is free at the point of use though with some exceptions. Apart from Child Benefit, most social security benefits are not provided universally. For most benefits the claimant has to have paid National Insurance contributions when working or undergo a "means test" to prove they are entitled to help from public funds.

10   The elderly receive a state retirement pension based on their National Insurance contributions. This pension on its own is not adequate to finance a comfortable old age. Many elderly people now have additional pensions. However, those with only the state pension can apply for means tested benefits to help with the cost of living.

Most elderly people stay in the house they grew old in. Many need personal care to
15   allow them to lead as normal a life as possible. Having assessed their needs, local authorities are responsible for organising care packages for the elderly. These packages involve personal care which includes regular visits by carers to help with washing, dressing and preparing meals. Elderly people who enter sheltered housing or a residential home also receive personal care.

20   In 2002, following the recommendations of the Sutherland Report, the Scottish Executive introduced free personal care for all elderly people in Scotland. In other parts of the UK, personal care is still means tested. Even so the majority of elderly people in England do receive free personal care with only the better off having to contribute to their care costs. Nursing care, like other forms of NHS medical care, is provided
25   without charge.

The effects of free personal care have been controversial. In Scotland, its take up rate has gone up dramatically, suggesting it is meeting a need but at a reported cost of over £150 million in 2005–2006. Critics argue that these resources are taking away from more pressing priorities and that the Scottish Executive should introduce means testing.

Newspaper Editorial

SOURCE B1:   SAY "NO" TO MEANS TESTING PERSONAL CARE!

Free personal care has been a Scottish success story. Our old people deserve it.
Throughout their working lives they paid contributions into a Welfare State they
believed would provide for them in their old age.

5
It is not realistic to claim that nursing and personal care can be separated. The
Sutherland Report was right to say that an elderly person with dementia in a residential
home should have their personal care funded in the same way as any elderly NHS
hospital patient. Furthermore, the majority of elderly people do not claim those
benefits which are means tested. Local authority tenants lose a smaller percentage of
their income than owner occupiers even though they are more likely to claim. In

10
England, elderly people with savings have to use them to pay for personal care. Why
should they be penalised for thrift? The English system is so complex that health
authorities have had to review all long term care cases and pay out £500 million to
elderly people who were wrongly assessed.

Free personal care is entirely within the original aims of the Welfare State. If its cost is

15
a problem then it can easily be solved. The Scottish Executive has the power to increase
Income Tax in Scotland by up to 3p in the pound. It should be prepared to do this for
the sake of our old folk rather than expose them to the terrible consequences of means
testing!

Patricia Sweeney

SOURCE B2:   SAY "YES" TO MEANS TESTING PERSONAL CARE!

Free personal care is not in line with the original aims of the Welfare State. It is not
sensible to have one benefit for the elderly paid out universally when others are subject
to conditions. Irrespective of where they live in the UK, the elderly should receive
identical treatment. Some people want free personal care provided throughout the UK.

5
However, this would cost £1 billion per year and use up resources that could be more
usefully spent elsewhere.

Many elderly people are comfortably off and well able to pay for their personal care.
Those who are less fortunate are already provided for. The elderly already get the
biggest share of government spending on benefits despite the fact that a higher

15
percentage of families with children live on very low incomes.

In Scotland, free personal care is not working. The Scottish Executive does not provide
local authorities with sufficient funding. There are too few places in local authority
residential homes. Places in private residential homes are too expensive for many. This
aggravates bed blocking in NHS hospitals at huge extra cost to the taxpayer.

20
Scottish politicians should accept they made a huge mistake when they introduced free
personal care for the elderly. There is no doubt that means testing represents best value.
It is time to stop spending millions of pounds on people who do not need financial help
and instead target resources on those who do.

Edwin Hughes

[Turn over for Source C on *Pages four* and *five*

SOURCE C: STATISTICAL INFORMATION

SOURCE C1: Estimated % increases within the UK population

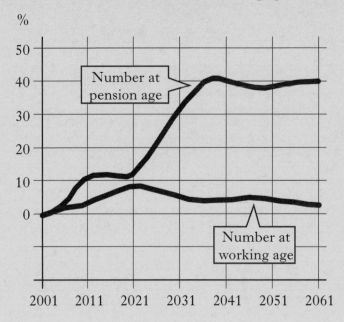

Source: House of Lords Economic Affairs Committee

SOURCE C2: Benefits and income for certain groups in the UK

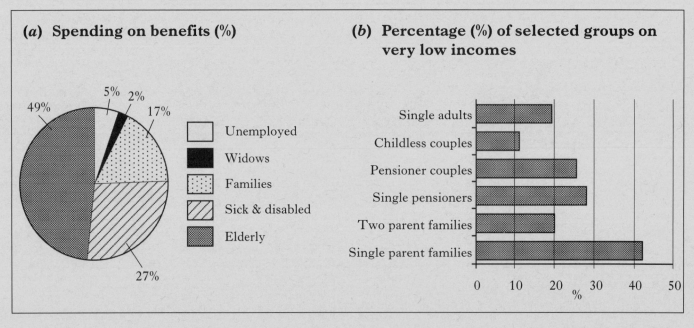

(a) Spending on benefits (%)

Unemployed
Widows
Families
Sick & disabled
Elderly

(b) Percentage (%) of selected groups on very low incomes

Adapted from Social Trends

SOURCE C3: Take up of means tested benefits by the elderly

	Claiming all their Entitlement	Claiming some Entitlement	Claiming no Entitlement	% Effects on Income*
Local Authority/ Housing Association tenant	78	15	8	−41·1
Owner occupier	45	10	45	−12·8
All pensioners	64	13	23	−25·6

* of not claiming full entitlement

Adapted from a Family Resources Survey

DECISION MAKING EXERCISE

QUESTIONS

Marks

Questions 1 to 3 are based on Sources A to C on pages 2–4. Answer Questions 1 to 3 before attempting Question 4.

In Questions 1 to 3, use only the Sources described in each question.

Question 1   *Use **only** Source C1 and Source A.*

Give evidence for and against the view in the newspaper editorial.

2

Question 2   *Use **only** Source C2(a), Source C2(b) and Source B2.*

To what extent has Edwin Hughes been selective in the use of facts?

4

Question 3   *Use **only** Source C3 and Source B1.*

To what extent does the evidence support Patricia Sweeney?

4

(10)

Question 4

Marks

DECISION MAKING TASK

You are a leading academic in the field of social policy. You have been asked to prepare a report for the Scottish Executive in which you recommend or reject the proposal to introduce means testing for the provision of personal care for elderly people in Scotland.

Your answer should be written in a style appropriate to a *report*.

Your report should:

*   recommend or reject the proposal to means test personal care for elderly people in Scotland

*   provide arguments to support your decision

*   identify and comment on any arguments which may be presented by those who oppose your decision

*   refer to all the Sources provided

    AND

*   <u>must</u> include relevant background knowledge.

The written and statistical sources which have been provided are:

SOURCE A: Caring for the Elderly

SOURCE B1:   Say "No" to Means Testing Personal Care!

SOURCE B2:   Say "Yes" to Means Testing Personal Care!

SOURCE C: Statistical Information

(20)

Total: 30 Marks

[END OF SPECIMEN QUESTION PAPER]

[BLANK PAGE]

X236/301

NATIONAL
QUALIFICATIONS
2007

TUESDAY, 22 MAY
9.00 AM – 10.30 AM

MODERN STUDIES
HIGHER
Paper 1

Candidates should answer **FOUR** questions:

- **ONE** from Section A

and

- **ONE** from Section B

and

- **ONE** from Section C

and

- **ONE OTHER** from **EITHER** Section A **OR** Section C

Section A: Political Issues in the United Kingdom.

Section B: Social Issues in the United Kingdom.

Section C: International Issues.

Each question is worth 15 marks.

SCOTTISH
QUALIFICATIONS
AUTHORITY
©

SECTION A—Political Issues in the United Kingdom

Each question is worth 15 marks

STUDY THEME 1A: DEVOLVED DECISION MAKING IN SCOTLAND

Question A1

The distribution of reserved and devolved powers means that the most important decisions for Scotland continue to be made at Westminster.

Discuss.

STUDY THEME 1B: DECISION MAKING IN CENTRAL GOVERNMENT

Question A2

To what extent can Parliament control the powers of the Prime Minister?

STUDY THEME 1C: POLITICAL PARTIES AND THEIR POLICIES (INCLUDING THE SCOTTISH DIMENSION)

Question A3

Assess the importance of party unity in achieving electoral success.

STUDY THEME 1D: ELECTORAL SYSTEMS, VOTING AND POLITICAL ATTITUDES

Question A4

The Additional Member System gives voters more choice and better representation than does First Past The Post.

Discuss.

SECTION B — Social Issues in the United Kingdom

Each question is worth 15 marks

STUDY THEME 2: WEALTH AND HEALTH INEQUALITIES IN THE UNITED KINGDOM

EITHER

Question B5

To what extent are the founding principles of the Welfare State being met?

OR

Question B6

To what extent do social and economic inequalities continue to exist in the UK?

[Turn over

SECTION C — International Issues
Each question is worth 15 marks

STUDY THEME 3A: THE REPUBLIC OF SOUTH AFRICA

Question C7

Its political system has all the features of a democracy but South Africa has become a one party state.

Discuss.

STUDY THEME 3B: THE PEOPLE'S REPUBLIC OF CHINA

Question C8

Critically examine the effects of social and economic reform in China.

STUDY THEME 3C: THE UNITED STATES OF AMERICA

Question C9

To what extent do ethnic minorities influence the outcome of elections in the USA?

STUDY THEME 3D: THE EUROPEAN UNION

Question C10

To what extent is there agreement amongst member states on EU social and economic policies?

STUDY THEME 3E: THE POLITICS OF DEVELOPMENT IN AFRICA

Question C11

With reference to specific African countries (excluding the Republic of South Africa):

Foreign aid alone is no guarantee of development.

Discuss.

STUDY THEME 3F: GLOBAL SECURITY

Question C12

Critically examine the effectiveness of international responses to threats to global security.

[END OF QUESTION PAPER]

X236/302

NATIONAL
QUALIFICATIONS
2007

TUESDAY, 22 MAY
10.50 AM – 12.50 AM

MODERN STUDIES
HIGHER
Paper 2

Summary of Decision Making Exercise

You are a social policy researcher. You have been asked to prepare a report for a committee investigating welfare provision in which you recommend or reject the proposal to introduce an Employment and Support Allowance (ESA).

Before beginning the task, you must answer a number of evaluating questions (Questions 1–3) based on the source material provided. The source material is:

SOURCE A: ESA will be fairer

SOURCE B: ESA will increase hardship

SOURCE C: Statistical Information

SCOTTISH
QUALIFICATIONS
AUTHORITY
©

SOURCE A: ESA WILL BE FAIRER

Incapacity Benefit is meant to provide an income for people who are unable to work because of medical reasons. It is the single most costly benefit that applies to people of working age. The number of people claiming Incapacity Benefit has grown to 2·7 million. Most, but not all of these claimants, are genuinely disabled or suffering

5   from a health condition that prevents them from working. In Scotland, over 300,000 people receive Incapacity Benefit. In Glasgow, one in five of those of working age claim this benefit. Incapacity Benefit increases after six months and again after a year. It is paid for life and may be accompanied by other benefits. Incapacity Benefit discourages people from seeking work. No wonder long-term sickness and disability is the most

10 common reason given by both men and women for not working. It is not just older workers who qualify for Incapacity Benefit – each month over a thousand teenagers claim it. We are encouraging welfare dependency at the expense of individual responsibility. Incapacity Benefit needs reform.

Our proposed Employment and Support Allowance (ESA) will be fairer to new

15 claimants and give the taxpayer better value for their money. It will pay more than Incapacity Benefit but new applicants will face rigorous medical tests to prove that they are entitled to it. Those judged capable of work will have to attend "work-focused interviews" and take part in "work-related activities". At these interviews employment advisers will be available to help place people in appropriate employment. Claimants

20 who refuse to attend for interview will have their payments cut. Those who take up employment will qualify for extra benefits. The practice of increasing benefits over time will be scrapped.

The UK already spends a greater percentage of its Gross Domestic Product (GDP) on schemes for disabled workers than any other country in the European Union. We are

25 determined to continue to move people from welfare into work. Our proposed reform should lead to a million fewer Incapacity Benefit claimants by 2016. The social and economic benefits of work to the individual are obvious. New technology ensures that work is now less physically demanding. Savings made from the reform of Incapacity Benefit will, of course, be welcome. However, our main aim is to return to the

30 fundamental principles of the welfare state. It is surely far better to help people into the workplace than to condemn them to a life on benefits!

Russell Barclay, Department for Work and Pensions (DWP) Spokesperson

SOURCE B: ESA WILL INCREASE HARDSHIP

In the UK today, more people than ever are in need of support from public funds. There are 7 million people of working age with either a mental or physical disability. Charities raise millions of pounds to plug the income and health gaps in the welfare state. They already spend more on the disabled than on any other group. Yet surely it is
5 the responsibility of the state – not charities – to support people in need. There may well be 2·7 million who claim Incapacity Benefit but the number actually receiving Incapacity Benefit fell from 1·9 million in 1995 to 1·7 million in 2004, as so many claimants are turned down. This shows how tough the rules are already.

Politicians should not complain about the cost of the welfare state, and certainly never
10 about Incapacity Benefit. During the 1980s, it was government policy to encourage people to claim Incapacity Benefit in order to hide the true level of unemployment. Now, the Government will increase hardship by discouraging people from claiming a benefit to which they should be entitled. Disability experts forecast big problems in deciding who is fit enough to work. Mistakes will be made. Many claimants will be
15 unable to cope with the stress of attending interviews. Others will be pressed into taking and keeping jobs for which they are neither physically nor mentally fit. It is disgraceful that those with disabilities, and other groups vulnerable to poverty, such as lone-parents, are being forced into employment situations that they are unable to cope with. "Welfare to Work" policies are clearly more about saving money than meeting needs.

20 We live in an unequal society where there are obstacles to employment for many disabled people. Around a million people who want to work cannot find jobs, as employers are reluctant to take on staff with disabilities or other health problems. UK Government spending on the sick and disabled is already lower than for any other group and a lower percentage of one-parent families receive Incapacity/Disability Benefit than any other
25 benefit. Effective laws to prevent discrimination against the disabled would be far more useful than making the rules for Incapacity Benefit even tougher. We fully support any proposals that help disabled people to get jobs but we totally oppose this proposed reform of Incapacity Benefit. An Employment and Support Allowance (ESA) will only lead to more social exclusion and undermine the collectivist principles of the welfare
30 state.

Irene Graham, Disability Support Group (DSG) Spokesperson

[Turn over for Source C on *Pages four* and *five*

SOURCE C: **STATISTICAL INFORMATION**

SOURCE C1: **Reasons given by people of working age for not working**

Male	Reasons	Female
%		%
37	Long-term sickness/disability	21
6	Looking after family/home	45
30	Student	19
13	Early retirement	4
14	Other	11

Source: Adapted from Labour Force Survey, Office for National Statistics

SOURCE C2:

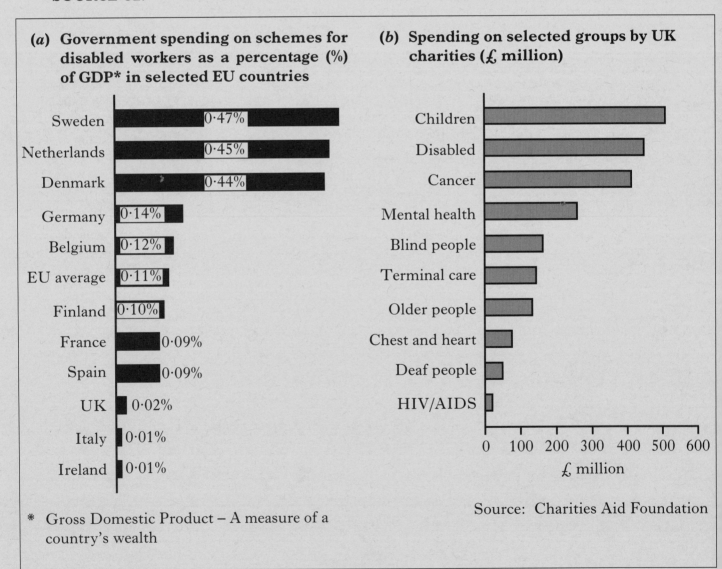

(a) **Government spending on schemes for disabled workers as a percentage (%) of GDP* in selected EU countries**

Sweden 0·47%
Netherlands 0·45%
Denmark 0·44%
Germany 0·14%
Belgium 0·12%
EU average 0·11%
Finland 0·10%
France 0·09%
Spain 0·09%
UK 0·02%
Italy 0·01%
Ireland 0·01%

(b) **Spending on selected groups by UK charities (£ million)**

Children
Disabled
Cancer
Mental health
Blind people
Terminal care
Older people
Chest and heart
Deaf people
HIV/AIDS

0 100 200 300 400 500 600
£ million

Source: Charities Aid Foundation

* Gross Domestic Product – A measure of a country's wealth

SOURCE C: (CONTINUED)

SOURCE C3:

(a) Percentage (%) share, by group, of UK Government benefit spending

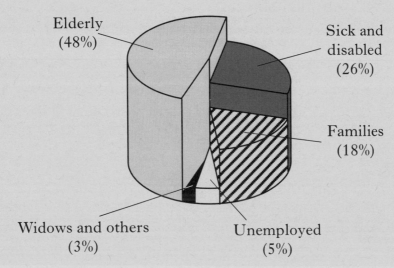

Source: Adapted from Department for Work and Pensions

(b) Percentage (%) of one-parent families receiving selected benefits

Benefit	(%)
Child	97
Working Families Tax Credit, Income Support **or** Minimum Income Guarantee	76
Incapacity/Disability	9
Council Tax	49
Housing	48

Source: Adapted from Family Resources Survey,
Department for Work and Pensions

[BLANK PAGE]

DECISION MAKING EXERCISE

QUESTIONS

Marks

Questions 1 to 3 are based on Sources A to C on pages 2–5. Answer Questions 1 to 3 before attempting Question 4.

In Questions 1 to 3, use only the Sources described in each question.

Question 1 *Use **only** Source C1 and Source A.*

To what extent does the evidence support Russell Barclay?   **3**

Question 2

(*a*) *Use **only** Source C2(a) and Source A.*

Why might Russell Barclay be accused of exaggeration?   **2**

(*b*) *Use **only** Source C2(b) and Source B.*

Why might Irene Graham be accused of exaggeration?   **2**

Question 3 *Use **only** Source C3(a), Source C3(b) and Source B.*

To what extent does the evidence support Irene Graham?   **3**

    (10)

Question 4

DECISION MAKING TASK

You are a social policy researcher. You have been asked to prepare a report for a committee investigating welfare provision in which you recommend or reject the proposal to introduce an Employment and Support Allowance (ESA).

Your answer should be written in a style appropriate to a *report*.

Your report should:

- recommend or reject the proposal to introduce an Employment and Support Allowance (ESA)

- provide arguments to support your decision

- identify and comment on any arguments which may be presented by those who oppose your decision

- refer to all the Sources provided

  AND

- **must** include relevant background knowledge.

The written and statistical sources which have been provided are:

SOURCE A: ESA will be fairer

SOURCE B: ESA will increase hardship

SOURCE C: Statistical Information

(20)

Total: 30 Marks

[END OF QUESTION PAPER]

[BLANK PAGE]

Official SQA Past Papers: Higher Modern Studies 2008

X236/301

NATIONAL
QUALIFICATIONS
2008

THURSDAY, 29 MAY
9.00 AM – 10.30 AM

MODERN STUDIES
HIGHER
Paper 1

Candidates should answer **FOUR** questions:

- **ONE** from Section A

and

- **ONE** from Section B

and

- **ONE** from Section C

and

- **ONE OTHER** from <u>**EITHER**</u> Section A <u>**OR**</u> Section C

Section A: Political Issues in the United Kingdom.

Section B: Social Issues in the United Kingdom.

Section C: International Issues.

Each question is worth 15 marks.

SECTION A—Political Issues in the United Kingdom
Each question is worth 15 marks

STUDY THEME 1A: DEVOLVED DECISION MAKING IN SCOTLAND

Question A1

Critically examine the role of local government in a devolved Scotland.

STUDY THEME 1B: DECISION MAKING IN CENTRAL GOVERNMENT

Question A2

Assess the effectiveness of pressure groups in influencing decision-making in Central Government.

STUDY THEME 1C: POLITICAL PARTIES AND THEIR POLICIES
(INCLUDING THE SCOTTISH DIMENSION)

Question A3

There are few policy differences between the main political parties.

Discuss.

STUDY THEME 1D: ELECTORAL SYSTEMS, VOTING AND POLITICAL
ATTITUDES

Question A4

Assess the influence of social class on voting behaviour.

SECTION B — Social Issues in the United Kingdom

Each question is worth 15 marks

STUDY THEME 2: WEALTH AND HEALTH INEQUALITIES IN THE UNITED KINGDOM

EITHER

Question B5

Assess the effectiveness of government policies to reduce gender and ethnic inequalities.

OR

Question B6

Critically examine the view that government, not individuals, should be responsible for health care and welfare provision.

[Turn over

SECTION C — International Issues
Each question is worth 15 marks

STUDY THEME 3A: THE REPUBLIC OF SOUTH AFRICA

Question C7

Assess the effectiveness of Black Economic Empowerment in reducing inequalities.

STUDY THEME 3B: THE PEOPLE'S REPUBLIC OF CHINA

Question C8

Critically examine the view that China is becoming a more democratic society.

STUDY THEME 3C: THE UNITED STATES OF AMERICA

Question C9

Assess the effectiveness of Congress and the Supreme Court in checking the powers of the President.

STUDY THEME 3D: THE EUROPEAN UNION

Question C10

Assess the impact of enlargement on the European Union.

STUDY THEME 3E: THE POLITICS OF DEVELOPMENT IN AFRICA

Question C11

With reference to specific African countries (excluding the Republic of South Africa):

Assess the importance of education and health care to successful development.

STUDY THEME 3F: GLOBAL SECURITY

Question C12

Critically examine the part played by the USA in achieving global security.

[END OF QUESTION PAPER]

X236/302

NATIONAL
QUALIFICATIONS
2008

THURSDAY, 29 MAY
10.50 AM – 12.05 PM

MODERN STUDIES
HIGHER
Paper 2

Summary of Decision Making Exercise

You are an expert on social policy. You have been asked to prepare a report for an all-party group of MSPs, in which you recommend or reject the proposal to make all prescriptions free in Scotland.

Before beginning the task, you must answer a number of evaluating questions (Questions 1–3) based on the source material provided. The source material is:

SOURCE A: Prescription Charges are a Danger to Health

SOURCE B: Prescription Charges are Necessary

SOURCE C: Statistical Information

SOURCE A: PRESCRIPTION CHARGES ARE A DANGER TO HEALTH

The Scottish Government is to be commended for its determination to phase out and eventually abolish prescription charges. Since first introduced, prescription charges have been kept ever since, except for a brief period of abolition in the 1960s. Although large numbers of prescriptions are dispensed free, the price per item is such that many
5   adults find it very difficult to pay.

Since April 2007, all patients registered with a Welsh GP, who get their prescriptions from a Welsh pharmacist, have been entitled to free prescriptions. There is no evidence that this has led to an increased demand for prescriptions in Wales. The suggestion that people ask for unnecessary prescriptions is ridiculous. The most common reasons for
10   not handing in a prescription are to do with cost—no one finds that they did not need it after all. Prescription charges prevent the sick from getting essential medicines. Being forced to decide which item on a prescription they can afford is one choice that patients can do without. The effects of this on individuals, and in the longer term on the National Health Service (NHS), should be obvious! Interrupting or delaying treatment
15   for just a few days can increase the risks to one's health. The long-term costs to the NHS become much greater because hospital treatment that could have been avoided becomes necessary.   GPs have become so concerned about the consequences of prescription charges that one in five has admitted to falsifying paperwork to ensure that vulnerable patients get free prescriptions.

20   The prescription charge is a tax on the sick and not at all in keeping with the founding principles of the NHS. Furthermore, it undermines any attempts to tackle the health divide in a society in which the link between deprivation and ill health has been clearly established. The pre-payment certificate only benefits those who can afford it. There is no way that patients on low incomes can afford to pay the required lump sum in
25   advance. The actual revenue gained from prescription charges is a tiny proportion of the estimated £10 billion budget for the NHS in Scotland. Making all prescriptions free in Scotland would be straightforward, effective and fair. <u>Free prescriptions would make a huge difference as to whether people would or would not go to a doctor.</u> There would be an immediate improvement in the health of the nation from which future generations
30   would only benefit.

Daphne Millar, Anti-Poverty Campaigner

SOURCE B: PRESCRIPTION CHARGES ARE NECESSARY

Within a few years of the creation of the NHS, a charge for each item on a prescription was introduced in response to the rising costs of medicines. However, children under 16 and men and women aged 60 and over get free prescriptions. Other categories of people are also entitled to exemption from NHS prescription charges. Around half of the
5   population qualify for free prescriptions. This results in 90% of dispensed prescription items being issued free of charge. For those who do have to pay, there is a system of pre-payment certificates. This gives unlimited prescriptions for up to twelve months for a one-off payment. Furthermore, almost two in every three medicines available on prescription can be bought more cheaply over the counter. Despite prescription charges,
10   the NHS has always enjoyed strong public support. In a recent survey on health care systems in European countries, the UK was one of the highest rated.

The UK Government intends to keep prescription charges in England. The Scottish Government must keep them too. It is estimated that in the financial year 2007–2008, prescription charges brought in a much-needed £46 million in revenue to the NHS in
15   Scotland. Such a sum buys a lot of health care, be it equipment or staff. Abolish charges, and the demand for unnecessary prescriptions will surely increase. GPs are concerned about the number of patients who consult them for no good medical reason. If charges are abolished, the number of patients asking doctors for unnecessary prescriptions will increase. This will put pressure on the drugs budget and may mean
20   delays in introducing life saving but expensive new drugs.

Abolishing prescription charges will not help those on low incomes. It will divert resources towards those on middle and upper incomes. Most people who have to pay can afford all of the items on their prescriptions and there is little support from health and community groups for completely abolishing prescription charges. Abolishing
25   prescription charges would have a bad effect on both the financing and performance of the NHS in Scotland. The resulting cutbacks in the provision of care would hit the poorest members of society the most. Prescription charges must be retained if the health gap is to be closed.

Tom Beattie, Health Economist

[Turn over for Source C on *Pages four* and *five*

SOURCE C: STATISTICAL INFORMATION

SOURCE C1:   Public opinion survey results

(a) Reasons patients gave for not handing in prescriptions

It cost less to buy the medicine over the counter	28%
It cost too much money (£6·85 per item)	25%
Health improved – did not need it after all	10%
I wanted to wait and see if I felt better	16%
I didn't feel I was prescribed the correct medicine	11%
I had some medicine left from the last time	5%
I forgot about it	5%

Source: Adapted from Consultation on Review of NHS Prescription Charges
(Scotland) 2007

(b) If all prescriptions became free, in what way would it influence your decision to go to the doctor?

% of people surveyed

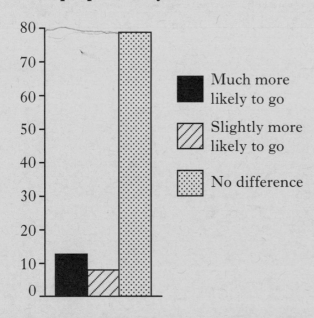

Source: Adapted from Consultation on Review of NHS Prescription Charges (Scotland) 2007

(c) In the past year, how many items on your prescriptions have you been able to afford?

% of people surveyed

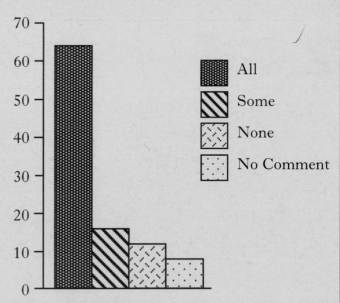

Source: Adapted from National Association of Citizens Advice Bureaux data 2001

SOURCE C: (CONTINUED)

SOURCE C2: How people rate their health care systems (perfect score 100)

Country	Score
Belgium	66
France	65
Germany	76
Hungary	58
Italy	48
Netherlands	80
Poland	41
Spain	61
Sweden	66
Switzerland	78
UK	60

Source: Adapted from *The Times*, June 2005

SOURCE C3: Results of consultation with health and community groups

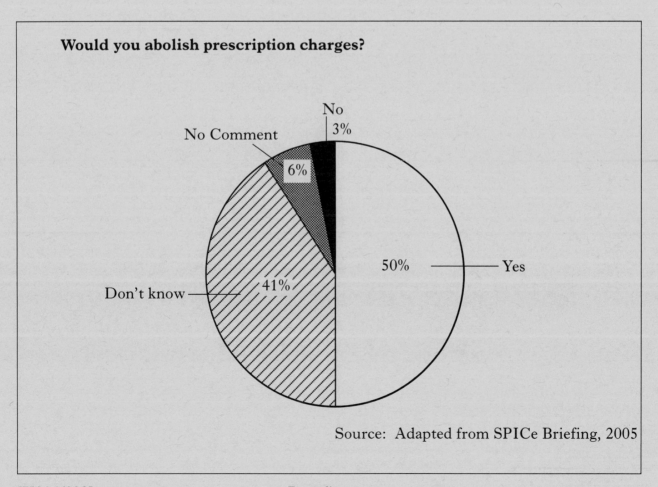

Would you abolish prescription charges?

No 3%

No Comment 6%

Don't know 41%

50% — Yes

Source: Adapted from SPICe Briefing, 2005

[BLANK PAGE]

DECISION MAKING EXERCISE

QUESTIONS

Marks

Questions 1 to 3 are based on Sources A to C on pages 2–5. Answer Questions 1 to 3 before attempting Question 4.

In Questions 1 to 3, use <u>only</u> the Sources described in each question.

Question 1   *Use* **only** *Source C1(a) and Source A.*

To what extent does the evidence support Daphne Millar?   3

Question 2

(*a*) *Use* **only** *Source C1(b) and Source A.*

Why might Daphne Millar be accused of exaggeration?   2

(*b*) *Use* **only** *Source C2 and Source B.*

Why might Tom Beattie be accused of exaggeration?   2

Question 3   *Use* **only** *Source C1(c) and Source C3 and Source B.*

To what extent does the evidence support Tom Beattie?   3

(10)

Question 4

Marks

DECISION MAKING TASK

You are an expert on social policy. You have been asked to prepare a report for an all-party group of MSPs, in which you recommend or reject the proposal to make all prescriptions free in Scotland.

Your answer should be written in a style of a *report*.

Your report should:

- recommend or reject the proposal to make all prescriptions free in Scotland

- provide arguments to support your decision

- identify and comment on any arguments which may be presented by those who oppose your decision

- refer to all the Sources provided

  AND

- **must** include relevant background knowledge.

The written and statistical sources which have been provided are:

SOURCE A: Prescription Charges are a Danger to Health

SOURCE B: Prescription Charges are Necessary

SOURCE C: Statistical Information

(20)

Total: 30 Marks

[END OF QUESTION PAPER]

[BLANK PAGE]

[BLANK PAGE]

[BLANK PAGE]

[BLANK PAGE]

[BLANK PAGE]

Acknowledgements

Leckie & Leckie is grateful to the copyright holders, as credited, for permission to use their material:
Profile Books Ltd for an extract from The Economist Pocket World in Figures (2005 Paper 2 Exercise 1 p 4);
The Times for the chart 'Cancer survival rates in selected countries' © NI Syndication (2005 Paper 2 Exercise 2 p 4);
The Economist for the graph 'Spending on state benefits in selected countries as a percentage of GDP' (2006 Paper 2 Exercise 1 p 5) and the chart 'Public Opinion Survey' adapted from the article 'The Politics of Choice' from The Economist (2006 Paper 2 Exercise 2 p 5).

The following companies/individuals have very generously given permission to reproduce their copyright material free of charge:
Her Majesty's Stationery Office for an extract from Social Trends
(2004 Paper 2 Exercise 2 p 4 and 2007 SQP Paper 2 p 4); Her Majesty's Stationery Office for a table, diagram and chart (2008 Paper 2 p 4 and p 5) ;The Department of Work and Pensions (2004 Paper 2 Exercise 1 p 4 and 2007 Paper 2 p 5); The Department of Health (2004 Paper 2 Exercise 2 p 4); HM Treasury (2004 Paper 2 Exercise 2 p 4); House of Lords Economic Affairs Committee (2007 SQP Paper 2 p 4); and Office for National Statistics (2007 Paper 2 p 4).
Mori for two graphs (2004 Paper 2 Exercise 1 p 4);
The Institute for Fiscal Studies for the graph 'Real annual average income growth under Labour 1997–2000' (2004 Paper 2 Exercise 1 p 4);
ISD Publications for the graph 'Numbers on NHS hospital waiting lists for more than 15 months' (2004 Paper 2 Exercise 2 p 4);
The Bank of England for two graphs from 2003 (2005 Paper 2 Exercise 1 p 5);
Newsquest Media Group for the graph 'NHS spending per head in the UK, 1998-2003', the illustration 'Waiting time targets report (Scotland)', the graph 'Emergency admissions to hospital in Scotland, (selected age groups). 1981-2002' and the graph 'NHS bed provision in the UK' adapted from The Herald June 2004 (2006 Paper 2 Exercise 2 pp 4–5);
Charities Aid Foundation for two graphs (2007 Paper 2 p 4);
The Times for a table June 2005 (2008 Paper 2 p 5).

© 2008 Scottish Qualifications Authority/Leckie & Leckie, All Rights Reserved
Published by Leckie & Leckie Ltd, 3rd Floor, 4 Queen Street, Edinburgh EH2 1JE
tel: 0131 220 6831, fax: 0131 225 9987, enquiries@leckieandleckie.co.uk, www.leckieandleckie.co.uk

Modern Studies Higher 2006
Paper 1

Section A

Study Theme 1

Decision Making in Central Government

Question A1

(a) Developed and exemplified answers may feature reference to:
- formation and leadership of HMG
- relationship with the Cabinet
- the Prime Minister's Office
- special advisers
- implications of party leadership
- control of the parliamentary time table
- legislative delivery of the party's manifesto promises – has a built in majority in all parliamentary committees
- relationship with and performance in parliament (including voting record), at PMQT and when appearing before the Liaison Committee
- representation of the UK on the world stage
- choice of date for general election
- patronage
- other relevant points.

(b) Developed, exemplified and balanced answers may feature reference to:
- importance of the media to pressure groups seeking to effect changes in either the law or policy
- highlighting of an issue by the media can trigger a demand for change that is taken on by the government
- media investigates and challenges government decisions
- negative exposure/poor performance in opinion polls may lead to alterations in policy
- media campaigns not always successful
- involvement of the press in single-issue campaigns
- although the press may be as biased as it likes (within the law), the broadcasting media are required to be impartial
- acknowledgement of the influence of the media through increased use of 'spin' and 'getting the message across', coupled with accusations of bias on the part of the BBC
- media influence on the voter's choice of decision-makers at election time
- other relevant points.

Study Theme 2

The Government of Scotland

Question A2

(a) Developed and exemplified answers may feature reference to:
- powers derived from the Scottish Parliament
- must provide mandatory services such as education and social work
- provision of discretionary/permissive services derived from the power a council has to spend limited funds in the interests of the local area and its inhabitants
- limited revenue raising powers
- duty to promote the economic, social and environmental well-being of the areas they administer
- responsibility to operate within Scottish Executive-set policy parameters
- must set performance targets for each service they provide
- should be open and accountable to the public in the areas they administer
- other relevant points.

(b) Developed, exemplified and balanced answers may feature reference to:
- creation of an 'accountable, open and accessible' Scottish Parliament with 129 elected members and the extent to which these criteria have been fulfilled
- effects of the electoral system on representation in the Scottish Parliament as well as the leadership and composition of the Scottish Executive
- the devolved powers – their administrative and legislative consequences
- the reserved powers – their significance
- impact of devolution on Scottish representation at Westminster and the office of Secretary of State for Scotland
- McConnell's "mission creep"; accused of meddling in affairs over which the Scottish Executive has no powers (air gun licensing, foreign policy, asylum seekers)
- demand for more devolution
- claim that devolution has undermined the status of local government
- other relevant points.

Modern Studies Higher 2006
Paper 1 (cont.)

Study Theme 3

Political Parties and their Policies

Question A3

(a) Developed and exemplified answers may feature reference to:

Conservative Party
- One type of membership.
- Constituency Associations select candidates and have responsibility for funding.
- Party Board is responsible for all aspects of the party outside Parliament.
- Party Forum allows members to contribute to policy-making.
- Annual Party Conference.
- Arrangements for leadership challenge and choice.
- Other relevant points.

Labour Party
- Two types of membership - individual and affiliated.
- Constituency Labour Parties formed from both delegate members and representatives from affiliated organisations; choose candidates for elections, raise funds and recruit new members; elect representatives to a General Committee.
- National Executive Committee composed of representatives from CLPs and other affiliated groups; Leader and Deputy Leader also members; meets monthly and is responsible for looking after party affairs and implementing conference decisions.
- Annual Conference - composed of delegates from each of the CLPs and affiliated organisations.
- Arrangements for leadership challenge and choice.
- Other relevant points.

Liberal Democrat
- Constituency Associations.
- The Federal Conference attended by elected representatives from each local party, organised around parliamentary constituencies; decides policy matters on national and 'English' issues.
- Federal Committees (executive, policy and conference) are made up of members of the Parliamentary Party, the 'state' Parties and councillors; one third of each must be female.
- Federal Policy Committee of which the party leader is a member, is responsible for the manifesto.
- Arrangements for leadership challenge and choice.
- Other relevant points.

Question A3 (continued)

(b) Developed, exemplified and balanced answers may feature reference to:
- Emerged from the May 2005 election with 6 out of 59 Scottish seats at Westminster (one more than it started out with)
- Won seats from Labour for the first time in a Westminster election since the 1970s
- Share of the vote dropped by 2% putting it in third place, in terms of both seats and vote share, behind Liberal Democrats' 22.6% and 11 seats
- Came 'second' in the 2003 Holyrood election with 27 (9 constituency and 18 list) seats. However it had lost 8 seats and polled its lowest share of the vote in recent years
- Has only 1 MEP
- Ended 2005 with 183 councillors (largest party in Dundee), having won 7 of the previous 9 local council by-elections, and gaining representation in all of the Lothian councils for the first time.
- Opinion divided on the significance of the Livingston (Westminster) and the Glasgow Cathcart (Holyrood) by-election results
- Impact of 'gradualist/fundamentalist' split on electoral success
- New Alex Salmond/Nicola Sturgeon leadership
- The Dunfermline & West Fife result
- Other relevant points

Study Theme 4

The Electoral System, Voting and Political Attitudes

Question A4

(a) Developed and exemplified answers may feature reference to:
- social class
- geographic location
- age
- gender
- ethnicity
- party affiliation
- issues
- party image/leader
- tactical voting
- apathy
- distinction between short and long term factors
- other relevant points.

Question A4 (continued)

(b) Developed, exemplified and balanced answers may feature reference to:
Other 'fairer' (PR) systems that
- produce a closer link between the share of votes and share of seats and thereby a more representative parliament
- give the voters more choice
- discourage tactical voting. Voters are encouraged to vote for their natural party of choice in the knowledge that every vote counts and is of equal weight
- give smaller parties more parliamentary representation
- bring an end to 'elected dictatorships'
- provide for a more consensus style of government with more voters getting some of what they want and less of what they do not want.

But whose 'fairness' is limited by
- threat to the MP-constituency link with no facility for by-elections
- promotion of coalitions with a relatively unpopular party have undue influence
- limitations on the involvement of the prospective voter in candidate selection
- voters being 'represented' by people no one actually voted for
- some candidates getting two chances to become representatives
- the delivery of compromise policies that no one voted for
- the 'accountability' issue
- other relevant points.

Section B

Study Theme 5

Income and Wealth in the United Kingdom

Question B5

(a) Developed and exemplified answers may feature reference to:

Traditional Marxist definition
- based on workplace relationships
- capitalist v working class
- classes in hostile relationship to one another, leading to overthrow of capitalism and creation of communist, classless society.

Institute of Practitioners in Advertising (IPA) classification
A   Higher managerial, administrative or professional
B   Intermediate managerial, administrative, or professional
C1 Supervisory or clerical, and junior managerial, administrative or professional

Question B5 (a) (continued)

C2 Semi skilled manual workers
D   Semi skilled and unskilled manual workers
E   State pensioners or widows (no earnings), casual, low paid, long term unemployed

Right Wing Theories of class eg Charles Moore's "underclass"
- modern capitalism has not led to communism but better lives for the working and middle classes
- creation of a "new" class, the "underclass", which lives a life of crime and "dependency" on state benefits.

Use of Traits: education, income, occupation etc
- Changes in class mobility
- Other relevant definitions.

(b) Developed and exemplified answers may feature reference to:
Gender
- evidence generated by EOC reports (Sex and Power: Who Runs Britain?)
- most women still earning almost £100 a week less than men and full time women employees receive, on average, 72% of what a man earns; gender pay gap rises in the city where the average wage for women is 58% of men's
- girls outperform boys at school and make up nearly half of the Scottish workforce yet they account for only 10% senior police posts, 18% secondary head teachers and 27% councillors in Scotland
- Government funded study in England found that sexist attitudes and concerns about balancing family and work continued to be "major barriers" to the ambitions of female teachers. In England 31% of secondary heads are women though 55% of secondary teachers are female
- 17 directors of the FTSE 100 companies in the UK are female (400 men); no British woman has headed a big British company although 44% of the workforce is female
- in professions that are going female (medicine, church, the law) the glass ceiling is giving way to glass partitions - women are concentrating in the less well paid sectors
- old fashioned "jobs for the boys"/gender stereotyping; unequal distribution of family responsibilities; failure of employers to carry out gender-related pay reviews
- gender gap in pensioner income
- recognition of need for new anti-discrimination laws
- high profile discrimination cases
- other relevant points.

Modern Studies Higher 2006
Paper 1 (cont.)

Question B5 (*b*) (continued)

OR

Race
- racial harassment and attacks
- institutional racism
- old fashioned racial prejudice
- economic inequality between minority ethnic and white population
- questions over underachievement of particular groups; boys of West Indian origin are the likelier to be excluded from school, and later unemployed, yet they start off at primary school with better literacy and numeracy skills than any other minority ethnic group
- Fawcett Society research evidence: highlighted the exclusion of black and minority ethnic women at every level in society
- other relevant points.

(*c*) Developed and exemplified answers may feature reference to:
- unemployed harassed via the JSA into accepting low paid work
- unemployed not harassed enough into work e.g. Glasgow's high numbers on Incapacity Benefit
- moves to reform Incapacity Benefit
- benefits system is too complicated and inefficient
- implications of means testing
- National Minimum Wage not high enough
- issue of 'overpayment' of tax credits; although CTC favours poorer families, it is paid to well-off ones as well
- work-life balance measures
- other relevant points.

Study Theme 6

Health Care in the United Kingdom

Question B6

(*a*) Developed and exemplified answers may feature reference to:
- publicity campaigns on smoking, alcohol, illegal substances, diet, sexually transmitted diseases, vaccinations
- publication of health related data
- Anticipatory Care Strategy (Scotland) - "on the road" clinics offering heart, blood pressure and other health checks at sporting events, in shopping centres and entertainment complexes; teams of health workers to track down "couch potatoes" and encourage them to go to their GPs and undergo health checks before they end up in hospital
- Expert Patients Programme (England) - sufferers of chronic illnesses offered training to become an "expert patient" able to

Question B6 (*a*) (continued)

understand and monitor changes in their condition; at present being piloted with a view to being introduced nationally in 2008
- charges used as an educative measure to make the point of the cost of treatment and to encourage the notion that prevention is better than cure
- initiatives seen as 'cost neutral' because of later surgical procedure savings
- self-help procedures
- other relevant points.

(*b*) Developed and exemplified answers may feature reference to:
- evidence drawn from government, independent and media generated reports
- differences in morbidity and mortality; class, gender, ethnicity
- geographical/location differences, including hospital league tables
- differences in survival rates from specific conditions
- other relevant points.

(*c*) Developed and exemplified answers may feature reference to:
- claims that primary health care is neglected in favour of hospitals
- retirements outstripping recruitment; opposition parties claim that Westminster Government targets to increase numbers of GPs running 4 years behind schedule; waiting times for appointments getting longer
- varying standards of provision - postcode prescribing
- effects of new GP contracts
- shortage of provision in some areas
- NHS 24 (NHS Direct); concerns that patients' lives are being put at risk by a service that costs £4.7m a year (Scotland) to run
- crisis in dentistry - shortage of dentists and consequences of deregistration for NHS patients; one in three Scots children going without dental care; breakdown of talks over Dental Action Plan
- claim that the commitment to provide free major eye checks for all who need them diverts resources from the needy
- concerns over the 'cinderella' services, for example, mental health
- other relevant points.

Section C

Study Theme 7

A Society in Change – South Africa

Question C7

(a) Developed and exemplified answers may feature reference to:
- written constitution
- President (elected by the National Assembly) is both Head of State and Head of Government and appoints a cabinet.
- Parliament: National Assembly (400) and National Council of Provinces (90) elected by system of proportional representation.
- Each province has a Provincial Legislature from which is elected a Premier, who appoints an Executive Council.
- Judiciary consists of the Constitutional Court, the Supreme Court, and the High Court.
- Advisory bodies of 'Traditional Leaders' at both national and provincial levels.
- Local government organised around a system of metropolitan, district and local municipalities.
- 16 parties represented in Parliament but ANC continues to dominate.
- 97 parties contested the 2006 local elections with the ANC polling the most votes in each of the nine provinces (although it lost its position of power in Cape Town).
- The main challenge to the ANC comes from the Democratic Alliance Party.
- Inkatha Freedom Party believes in a federal system with strong provinces and a weak central government.
- Other relevant points.

(b) Developed, exemplified and balanced answers may feature reference to:
Education:
- Continues to account for one of the biggest shares of the national budget.
- Over 90% of South Africa's learners are now in school.
- Pass rates continue to improve.
- Qualifications of teachers have improved but many remain poorly trained.
- Pupil/teacher ratio has reduced but still relatively high.
- School and classroom building programme.
- School access to water (66%) and sanitation (84%) has improved.
- Expansion of state-funded National Student Financial Aid Scheme.
- Illiteracy rates falling but still high at around (30%) of adults over 15 years of age.

Question C7 (b) (continued)

- Students continue to be (illegally) suspended from schools for not paying fees.
- Effects of ill-health and AIDS/HIV.
- Other relevant points.

Housing
- Despite almost 1.5 million new homes built since 1994, still well short of original target for 2005.
- Percentage of home-owners has risen.
- The National Housing Finance Corporation and the National Housing Subsidy Programme help finance housing purchases.
- Government's low cost housing programme supports local labour and those who prefer to build their own homes.
- Many households remain without running water/electricity.
- Millions continue to live in squalid, disease-ridden shanties in informal settlements.
- Unemployment and low income remain barriers to people being adequately housed.
- Other relevant points.

Land Ownership
- Implementation of land ownership programme in the hands of the Land Claims Commission and the Land Claims Court.
- Agricultural workers on commercial farms are now entitled to protection from eviction and have security of tenure.
- Grants given to the poor and disadvantaged to help them buy land.
- Land transfer (30% by 2015) incomplete. Whites still own 80% of the land.
- Between 1994 and 2004 only 35% of rural land had been transferred from white ownership to black.
- 13 million people in the old homelands still own no land and nearly 40, 000 land restitution programmes waiting to be settled.
- Landless People's Movement (LMP) tried to organise a boycott of the 2004 elections in protest at the slow progress of the programme.
- Some provinces have introduced training programmes for black farmers to equip them with the skills required to become commercial farmers.
- In response to increasing violence against farmers and their families, the Government has introduced a Rural Protection Plan.
- Difficulties in balancing the interests of wealthy white farmers, who make a significant contribution to the country's economy, with those desperate for land.
- Many white farmers using the "willing buyer, willing seller" principal on which the programme is based to delay land transfer.
- Other relevant points.

Modern Studies Higher 2006
Paper 1 (cont.)

Study Theme 8

A Society in Change – China

Question C8

(a) Developed and exemplified answers may feature reference to:
- Incomes have risen in the cities, particularly in the coastal areas.
- Unprecedented access to consumer goods in urban areas; demand for cars increased by 56% in 2002 and by 75% in 2003 (before slowing down when the government tightened the rules on credit for car purchases).
- Growth in Yuan millionaires/billionaires as a consequence of changes to economic structures and financial rules.
- Less marked improvement in income and access to consumer goods and better housing in rural areas.
- "Document Number One" (December 2004) called for an increase in subsidies and greater government investment in agriculture to boost rural incomes.
- Present (rich urban) generation of 'only children' are the first to acquire big spending power; they have grown up enjoying enormous material comforts compared with their parents' generation.
- Official aim is to create a "well-to-do-society" with a per capita income of $5000 pa by 2020; acceptance that this standard will not match that of the West but it will nonetheless be a huge advance on the present figure.
- Success of the "great development of the west" policy.
- Relaxation of social controls made necessary by the decision to encourage private enterprise.
- Other relevant points.

(b) Developed, exemplified and balanced answers may feature reference to:
Social Reform
- Relaxation of the hukou (work permit system).
- Private ownership of land and business welcomed and encouraged.
- Relaxation of the One Child Policy.
- Better rights for women.
- Development of private health and education services.
- Gradual changes to the judicial system

Question C8 (b) (continued)

Political Reform discouraged
- President Hu's continued crackdown on pro-democracy movement.
- Democracy remains out of bounds as does the formation of any organised political group.
- Hu heads of all three branches of power - party, state, military; analysts claim that he sees his role as saving one-party rule, not ending it.
- CPC remains open to only 5-6% of the Chinese population; membership is by invitation only; allegations of cronyism/nepotism; adherence to CP decisions mandatory.
- Strict censorship and control of the media extends to cyberspace.
- Use of secret police and network of informers.
- Leaders of Democratic Party in Hong Kong not allowed to cross the 'border'.
- Since the 1980s, the country's 800, 000 villages have been regularly electing their own committee leaders but the Party remains firmly in control.
- Demands to extend the village election system to the townships (the lowest level of government after the villages) have been ignored.

However
- In 2005 it was announced that all of Sichuan's township level CP committees would be "required in principle" to hold democratic elections for Party chiefs in December (instead of them being appointed by secretive committee); voting would be confined to party members.
- Move to promote internal Party reform is seen as being designed to placate pro-democracy reformers, but more importantly, to reduce rural instability due to the heavy-handedness of local officials.
- Experiments with direct elections in a few urban areas at neighbourhood committee level with 'independents' being allowed to stand.
- Divisions within the Party over how to allow the people to take part in politics without causing a Soviet-style collapse.
- As agreed, half of Hong Kong's legislative council (Legco) are directly elected but any move to introduce greater democracy in Hong Kong will require clearance from the CPC.
- Media encouraged to investigate low-level social issues and corruption.
- Other relevant points.

Study Theme 9

Ethnic Minorities in the USA

Question C9

(a) Developed and exemplified answers may feature reference to:
  - Growth of the black middle class and in their number of CEOs in blue chip firms, and in the top ranks of the armed forces.
  - Average earnings for black females now 95% white level; for black males it is 72%.
  - Black political representation.
  - Black successes in sport, the entertainment industries, etc.
  - Hispanic economic, social and political success.
  - Asian economic, social and political success.
  - Other relevant points.

(b) Developed, exemplified and balanced answers may feature reference to:
  - Since re-election Bush has come under intense pressure to do something about immigration - from both sides in the debate: no longer a 6 state issue but a 50 state issue.
  - Restrictionists want fewer legal immigrants, a tougher border and harsher treatment for illegals.
  - Politicians from the border states paint a picture of mounting anarchy
  - Claim that immigrants take American jobs and/or become a burden on taxpayer-provided services; their acceptance of low-pay drives wage rates down generally.
  - "Minuteman project" (Arizona) to deter would be illegal immigrants
  - California's "Operation Gatekeeper".
  - Proposition 200 (Arizona) to prohibit any illegal immigrant from getting access to government benefits widely supported (including 47% of Latino voters).
  - Immigration seen as a threat to national security.
  - Liberalisers want to bow to economic reality and regularise the current situation through guest worker regulations.
  - Positive contribution to the economy made by immigrants.
  - Business opposes the choice between breaking the law and going out of business.
  - Trade Unionists see immigrants as potential recruits.
  - Reaction to Kennedy-McCain Bill.
  - Other relevant points.

Study Theme 10

The European Union

Question C10

(a) Developed and exemplified answers may feature reference to:
Commission
  - Brussels based members appointed by the national governments of each member state.
  - Each commissioner is responsible for a particular area of policy; each policy area has a director-general and staff to carry out and oversee policy.
  - Acts as the EU's executive; decisions taken on a corporate responsibility basis.
  - Manages EU policies and funds; is guardian of the treaties setting up the EU; has investigative powers; can impose fines on those who breach competition rules; can bring member states before the Court of Justice for obligation defaulting.
  - Other relevant points.
Council of Ministers
  - Brussels based Members are government ministers from each member state; meetings are attended by different ministers according to the agenda; presidency rotates every 6 months.
  - Discusses proposals put forward by the Commission and ensures that national interests are represented.
  - Decides what form these proposals should take, amends them if necessary and decides whether or not proposals should become law; many decisions taken behind closed doors.
  - Ministers may address the Parliament.
  - Other relevant points.
Parliament
  - Members are directly elected for a five year term on a member state basis; sit in political as opposed to national groupings; enlargement has seen membership increase to 732 although for a short time there were 788.
  - May veto draft legislation of the Commission; may scrutinise spending, reject nomination of a new president of the Commission, dismiss the Commission with a two-thirds majority vote of censure, and has the power of veto over new EU members and association agreements.
  - Co-decision powers.
  - May request legislative proposals from the Commission on specific issues; may propose an amendment through an absolute majority vote; may give an opinion on the Council's choice of President.
  - Other relevant points.

Modern Studies Higher 2006
Paper 1 (cont.)

Question C10 (continued)

(b) Developed, exemplified and balanced answers may feature reference to:
- Ten new members joined in May 2004.
- A broader, more effective cooperation in dealing with challenges such as environmental pollution and organised crime.
- Opportunities for businesses to develop new markets and new economies of scale.
- Collective GDP might overtake that of the USA.
- Between 2004 and 2005, the economies of the new members grew roughly 2-4 times as fast as the euro-zone average, despite fears that their industry would be choked by regulations and their agriculture ruined by the opening of markets.
- Manufacturers in new member states appear to have done unexpectedly well out of open borders and farmers have gained from subsidies and increased demand.

However
- Concerns over demands on structural funds.
- Fears that new, poorer regions will lower the EU's average income and disqualify some present members' regions from aid.
- The issue of economic migrants; new members have not automatically been given the freedom to work in most EU countries; only the UK, Ireland and Sweden have fully opened their labour markets; however some workers from central Europe are entering western labour markets illegally.
- Newcomers must meet further tests before they can join the single currency; their farmers get smaller direct subsidies from EU funds starting at 25% of the payments made to farmers in the 15 "old" members (a money saving measure meant to speed farm restructuring).
- Further EU enlargements; Bulgaria and Romania seem set (but not guaranteed) to join in 2007; Turkey accepted as a candidate; Albania, Bosnia, Croatia, Macedonia, Serbia and Montenegro promised in principle that they can join when they are ready.
- Other relevant points.

Study Theme 11

Global Security

Question C11

(a) Developed and exemplified answers may feature reference to:
- Over fifty years of peace in Europe for member states.
- Has delivered on its promise to defend Western Europe from communist encroachment.
- Success of Partnership for Peace and NATO-Russia Council.
- Expansion of membership.
- Establishment of Rapid Reaction force.
- Promotion of common operating procedures, technical standards and rule of engagement.
- Support for democracy in former communist countries.
- Peacekeeping in conjunction with the UN (Bosnia, Kosovo, Macedonia).
- Involvement in Afghanistan.
- Development of counter terrorism strategies.
- Other relevant points.

(b) Developed, exemplified and balanced answers may feature reference to:
- Criticism of UN involvement in the Congo and Somalia.
- Failed to prevent US-led war against Saddam Hussein; did not intervene in Rwanda, Darfur, or Kosovo.
- Security Council (+veto) built on the global order of 1945.
- Reform a priority for Kofi Annan since 1997; Brahimi Report (2000) and more recently Annan's "In Larger Freedom" report leading to 2005 proposals for reform - "an important step forward" (Annan): "the first steps" (Bush)
- Security Council enlarged from 15 to 24 with 6 new non-veto wielding permanent members.
- Introduction of new guidelines for the authorisation of military action.
- An agreed definition of terrorism that denies any exemption for "freedom fighters" like those in Chechnya and Palestine.
- Replace most of the Human Rights Commission with a smaller, elected HR Council.
- A responsibility to intervene to protect civilians from genocide or other atrocities.
- A new intergovernmental peace-building commission to help prevent "post conflict societies", like Congo, becoming failed states.
- Confirmation of a nation's right to launch a "pre-emptive" strike in the face of an "imminent" strike without going to the Security Council.
- Other relevant points.

Study Theme 12

The Politics of Food

Question C12

(a) Developed and exemplified answers may feature reference to:
- Good at small projects: handle these well and are sensitive to the needs of local people, involving them in decisions about food production and distribution.
- Strong emphasis on the importance of food security; encourage development of a food system that operates efficiently by providing enough food to eat, sufficient seeds to plant and an adequate supply of water for irrigation.
- Advice on farming and environmental improvements; encourage direction of funding towards afforestation to combat desertification.
- Campaigns to ensure land ownership.
- Early warning systems to monitor food supplies.
- Response to emergencies; feeding centres, lending of livestock, provision of transport.
- Cash for work and food for work schemes.
- Work closely with many UN programmes and agencies, including the World Food Programme.
- Campaigns to ban mines and clear minefields, and to cancel debt (if link to food production clearly established).
- Other relevant points.

(b) Developed, exemplified and balanced answers may feature reference to:
- Consequences of armed conflict between and within states.
- Alleged government involvement in kleptocracy, corruption and mismanagement of resources.
- Issue of land tenure and consequences of land reform policies (Zimbabwe).
- Initial refusal to admit to need (Niger); refusal of food aid (Zambia).
- Debt accumulation and policies (cash crops, taxation) to finance repayments.
- Insufficient investment in infrastructure to allow ease of movement of food from area of surplus to areas of shortage (Mozambique).
- Link between good governance and receipt of aid
- Negative consequences of some forms of aid.
- Internationally imposed terms of trade.
- Bad weather – particularly lethal consequences for countries during, or just after, armed conflict.
- Other relevant points.

Modern Studies Higher
Paper 2 – Decision Making Exercise 1 2006

1. (a) David McQueen states that the share of the population taken up by each age group in the over sixty-fives is set to keep on increasing for the foreseeable future.
Source C1 shows this to be true for those aged 75+ but not for those aged 65-74.

(b) Lisa Newman states that in relation to our European and non-European competitors, our state benefits take up a smaller share of our Gross National Product.
Source C2 shows that our benefits take up a smaller share than, for example, France or Germany, but take up a larger share than, for example, Canada or the USA.

2. (a) David McQueen states that an overwhelming majority of the over-50s intend to remain in paid employment well past any retirement date.
Source C3 shows that he is exaggerating as only 50% of over-50s plan to stay in work beyond retirement age.

(b) Lisa Newman states that most companies also have policies in place to deal with ageist attitudes in the workplace.
Source C3 shows that only 32% of companies have a policy to deal with ageism.

3. David McQueen states that they could now retire with dignity whereas Lisa Newman states that they would leave with the sack instead of a presentation and goodwill.

4. *Credit will be given to*:
- An introduction that indicates an awareness of the role to be adopted and makes a clear recommendation.
- Developed arguments in support of the recommendation.
- Identification of, comment on and rebuttal of counter arguments.
- Synthesis of Source material.
- Provision and use of appropriate background knowledge.
- A style appropriate to a report (sub-headings, chapters, etc).
- An overall conclusion.

Arguments for the proposal may feature:
- Possibility of increased financial burden on a reduced workforce.
- Legal entitlement to work.
- Helps provide for future financial security.
- Changes in lifestyle.
- Monitoring and evaluation methods to 'retire' unsuitable workers already in place.
- Increase in tax revenues/decrease in benefit expenditure.

Modern Studies Higher
Paper 2 – Decision Making Exercise 1
2006 (cont.)

4. (continued)

Arguments against the proposal may feature:
- Cost to GDP unlikely to change in the future.
- Costs involved in employing older workers.
- Existing flexible attitude to working beyond retirement.
- Importance of a balanced, dynamic workforce.
- Social inclusion policies have helped minimise employment record gaps.
- The requirement to maintain a competitive edge.

Credit will be given to background knowledge, developed from source material references to:

Source A:
- a demographic time bomb (Line 1)
- a variety of factors have made it difficult … to save for their future (Lines 11/12)
- choice in other areas of social policy (Line 24).

Source B:
- ageist attitudes in the workforce (Line 12)
- gaps in their employment record (Lines 20)
- social inclusion policies (Line 21).

"Original" background knowledge may feature:
- Problems of funding the welfare state and the pensions crisis.
- Existence of poverty (including pensioner poverty) in the UK.
- Government schemes to combat social exclusion.
- Increased use of means testing.
- Other relevant points.

Modern Studies Higher
Paper 2 – Decision Making Exercise 2
2006

1. The Editor states that centres have had a huge effect on waiting lists whereas Euan states their overall effect has been slight.

2. (*a*) The Editor states that despite spending more per person on health care, the Scottish NHS has achieved none of its waiting time targets.
   Source C1(a) shows that Scotland does spend more but Source C1(b) shows that - though others have not – the target for day patient care has been met.

   (*b*) Euan Ross states that in Scotland there has been no rise in emergency admissions and that the Scottish NHS is better off for beds than the English NHS.
   Source C2(a) shows that emergency admissions have risen but Source C2(b) shows that Scotland has higher bed provision per 1000 people than England.

3. Euan Ross states that people totally reject the notion that having more choice over where they are treated is important.
   Source C3 shows that 63% of the public say it is very/fairly important.

4. *Credit will be given to*:
   - An introduction that indicates an awareness of the role to be adopted and makes a clear recommendation.
   - Developed arguments in support of the recommendation.
   - Identification of, comment on and rebuttal of counter arguments.
   - Synthesis of Source material.
   - Provision and use of appropriate background knowledge.
   - A style appropriate to a report (sub-headings, chapters, etc).
   - An overall conclusion.

   Arguments for the proposal may feature:
   - Need to improve NHS efficiency, reduce waiting lists, give taxpayers best value.
   - English experience of these centres has been positive.
   - Continues theme of public-private co-operation.
   - Centres likely to bring new staff from abroad.
   - Allows NHS hospitals to concentrate on the more difficult problems.
   - Costs are cheaper than conventional private hospitals.

4. (continued)

Arguments against the proposal may feature:

- Around half of operations done by new centres could have been carried out by NHS hospitals.
- Loss of case load has a negative effect on the NHS.
- NHS staff effectively forced into the private sector.
- Creeping privatisation of the NHS.
- Increase in health inequalities.
- Private providers 'cherry pick' the NHS.
- Does not answer the real problems that confront the NHS.

Credit will be given to background knowledge, developed from source material references to:

Source A:

- free at the point of use (Line 3)
- another beneficial example of co-operation between the NHS and private sector (Lines 9/10)
- waiting time targets (Lines 26/27).

Source B:

- privatisation of health care (Line 15/16)
- inequality of health care (Lines 20)
- health care efficiency, … management, … investment (Line 27/28).

"Original" background knowledge may feature:

- Issue of waiting lists and waiting times in Scotland. Claims by the Scottish Executive that it has been successful in dealing with these, disputed by opposition parties.
- Political detail – different priorities for Blairites in England compared to traditional Labour in Scotland.
- Argument that Scotland has different health needs compared to England – relatively more poverty/effects of remoteness/scattered population – and other priorities.
- Evaluation of other English NHS reforms.
- Other relevant points.

Modern Studies Higher Specimen Paper 1 2007

SECTION A – Political Issues in the United Kingdom

Study Theme 1A: Devolved Decision Making in Scotland

Question A1

Developed, exemplified, balanced and analytical answers may refer to:

- local authorities have a duty to promote the economic, social and environmental well-being of the areas that they administer
- main functions are those associated with the delivery of the services for which they have been made responsible
- mandatory services, education, social work, must be provided
- discretionary/permissive services are derived from the power a council has to spend limited funds in the interests of the local area and its inhabitants
- the Scottish Parliament is responsible for Scottish local government
- Scottish Executive sets the parameters for most policies that councils have responsibility to deliver. Sets targets of councils using 'performance indicators' and council performance is monitored via Accounts Commission/Audit Scotland. Takes action where there is evidence of malpractice
- local authorities rely upon the Scottish Executive for most of their funding
- sources from which local authorities may raise money to finance their functions and the power of the Scottish Parliament to limit/ring fence these
- recent disagreements between local authorities and the Scottish Executive
- the UK Parliament and the Block Grant
- significance of 'reserved' powers in relation to promoting the economic, social and environmental well-being of the local area
- other relevant points.

Study Theme 1B: Decision Making in Central Government

Question A2

Developed, exemplified, balanced and analytical answers may refer to:

- pressure groups are, in many cases, unelected, unaccountable organisations with a relatively small active membership
- actions of some have been outside the law
- perceived disproportionate influence of insider groups
- concerns over financial links between some pressure groups and decision makers
- permit dialogue between governed and the government between elections

Modern Studies Higher
Specimen Paper 1
2007 (cont.)

Question A2 (continued)

- provide government with information and expertise
- articulate and defend minority interests
- check the possible abuse of power
- compete for policy adoption and/or change
- provide the expertise, knowledge and funding to get information from government
- many use the wide range of methods acceptable in a representative democracy
- other relevant points.

Study Theme 1C: Political Parties and their Policies (including the Scottish Dimension)

Question A3

Developed, exemplified, balanced and analytical answers may refer to:

Many areas of agreement, with a general consensus over extra funding for schools, reducing crime and keeping taxes for most about the same. Areas of difference include:

Education – England and Wales

Labour:
- schools given greater freedom to change curriculum, borrow money and set teachers' pay
- creation of 200 state-funded independent city academies; good schools can expand as long as they don't harm others
- local authorities recast as quality controllers, not direct suppliers; Labour to spend £77 billion by 2009/10.

Conservative:
- up to 600000 extra school places created to give parents more choice ('Right to Choose' package)
- independent schools to get state funding to about £5500 per pupil; every school would be given grant-maintained status; schools able to set own admissions policies and appeals panels for expelled pupils would be abolished; Conservatives to spend £62 billion overall by 2009/10.

Liberal Democrat:
- higher spending on education; smaller class sizes; scrap tuition fees.

Education-Scotland

Labour:
- no city academies; schools to remain under local authority control although more spending devolved to head teachers; curriculum to be broadened and made more flexible to cope with individual needs; school expansion plans and budgets still to be governed by local authorities; possible new 'experimental' schools to try out new ideas such as different school days or non-professional teachers.

Question A3 (continued)

Conservative:
- empower head teachers to exclude violent or disruptive pupils; encourage more choice of specialist schools; give schools greater freedom to set their own priorities.

Liberal Democrat:
- extend childcare schemes; increase out-of-school activities.

SNP:
- guarantee nursery place of at least 16 hours per week for every 3 and 4 year old; progressively cut class sizes; greater specialisation within comprehensive system; abolish Graduate Endowment Scheme and replace student loans with student grants.

Law and Order

Labour:
- community policing with dedicated policing teams of officers and community support officers focused on local priorities; increase the number of police officers; extend electronic tagging and restriction of liberty orders, parental orders to make parents responsible for their children.

Conservative:
- stiffer sentences for drug dealers and fast track prosecution; back zero tolerance; a 'more visible' crime fighting presence; take persistent young offenders off the streets; ensure criminals actually serve the sentences given out by courts.

Liberal Democrat:
- oppose ID cards; 1000 extra police officers; more resources to crime prevention/reduce re-offending.

SNP:
- oppose ID cards; more community policing; encourage alternatives to prison; fairer fines regime.

Taxation

Labour:
- no rise in personal taxation; increased public expenditure to be paid from efficiency savings.

Conservative:
- overall commitment to reducing tax burden but review of taxation and scope for tax cuts if possible.

Liberal Democrat:
- higher taxes on wealthiest (over £100000 pa); local income tax to replace Council Tax.

SNP:
- replace Council Tax with local income tax; introduction of a more progressive tax system.

Other relevant points.

Study Theme 1D: Electoral Systems, Voting and Political Attitudes

Question A4

Developed, exemplified, balanced and analytical answers may refer to:

- the broadcasting media, the press and the Internet
- social class
- region
- age
- religion
- ethnicity
- issue voting
- tactical voting
- rational choice model
- opinion polls
- electoral system and issue of 'effectiveness' of voting
- turnout for different levels of election
- other relevant points.

SECTION B – Social Issues in the United Kingdom

Study Theme 2: Wealth and Health Inequalities in the United Kingdom

Question B5

Developed, exemplified, balanced and analytical answers may refer to:

- founding principles of the Welfare State
- statistical evidence from both government-generated reports and independent health research in relation to morbidity and mortality
- low income linked to unhealthy lifestyles and high stress levels
- those at the lowest end of the social spectrum have the highest consumption of 'junk food' (getting the maximum amount of calories for their money) and lowest of fruit and vegetables
- people on low incomes cannot afford and seldom have access to shops selling good food
- better off can afford better diets, leisure activities that promote good health, better housing and safer environments
- middle and professional classes more likely to consult health professionals, know how to get the best out of the system, and follow positive health promotion advice
- twice as many women in bottom social class are obese compared with the top group
- 42% of unskilled workers smoke compared with 15% of professional males
- unskilled men have a shorter life expectancy overall
- effects of unemployment
- better off can afford the option of private health care
- experiences of black and minority ethnic groups
- other relevant points.

Study Theme 2: Wealth and Health Inequalities in the United Kingdom

Question B6

Developed, exemplified, balanced and analytical answers may refer to:

- national government legislation and local government initiatives to reduce discrimination against women and to encourage family-friendly working practices
- between 1996/7 and 2003/4 women's total individual income increased from 46% of men's to 53%. Individual income for women rose 31% in real terms, more than twice as fast as the 13% increase for men
- evidence of both 'occupational segregation' (the tendency for women to be employed in lower paid sectors) and a failure of employers to carry out gender-related pay reviews
- recent changes in legislation to make it easier for women to bring and win sexual discrimination cases
- despite recent growth in women earning top salaries (particularly in the City), their salaries still tend to be lower than those of men doing the same job; they hold fewer top jobs than men and are less likely to be promoted than men
- extent of exclusion among black and minority ethnic women
- introduction of paternity leave
- raising of state pension age for women to 65 to bring it into line with that for men
- the women's lobby and the EOC continue to campaign for the DTI to put more pressure on employers to promote equality between men and women
- women hold less than 10% of the most senior positions in many areas of British public life
- claim that the barriers to breaking through the 'glass ceiling' are down but a lot of women choose not to because they want to live and work differently
- campaigns for more health spending on screening men for treatable medical conditions
- other relevant points.

SECTION C – International Issues

Study Theme 3A: The Republic of South Africa

Question C7

Developed, exemplified, balanced and analytical answers may refer to:

- groups still tend to live apart despite no longer being forced to
- poverty rate highest for Blacks (56·3%) and lowest for Whites (6·9%)
- Blacks constitute the poorest group of the population, making up over 90% of the 21·9 million poor
- Whites still own 80% of land; land transfer still incomplete
- 22% Blacks without schooling whereas only 4% Whites are

Modern Studies Higher
Specimen Paper 1
2007 (cont.)

Question C7 (continued)

- unemployment highest for Blacks (50%)
- lower unemployment for Asians due to higher completion rate of Grade 12 schooling
- new 'poor' Whites come almost entirely from the Afrikaner community who make up 60% of the white population
- Whites control 90% of the economy
- Black economic empowerment (BEE)
- existence of black elite reflects no fundamental change in economic power
- increased access to fresh water, electricity and homes for many Blacks
- claims that Blacks are getting poorer while Whites are getting richer
- recent increase in the Gini coefficient
- health differences
- impact of crime
- gender inequalities
- other relevant points.

Study Theme 3B: The People's Republic of China

Question C8

Developed, exemplified, balanced and analytical answers may refer to:

- social controls have been loosened and unprecedented economic freedom has been allowed
- increased legal representation
- reduction in waiting time for those qualified to have a second child
- dismantling of the danwei
- relaxation of work permit system (hukou)
- changes to economic structures/financial rules (eg access to capital)
- growing urban affluence
- growth of middle classes with accompanying lifestyles; right to own private property now written into Constitution; wealth creation is part of being a good Communist
- 'Document Number One' aimed at boosting rural incomes (Dec 2004) called for an increase in subsidies and greater government investment in agriculture
- Official aim to create 'well-to-do-society' with per capita annual income of $5000 by 2020; acceptance that this standard will not match West but nonetheless a huge advance as annual per capita income in 2003 was $1090
- model of Russia's transition to capitalism not seen as a good one
- carefully controlled experiments in democracy, eg in Ya'an-a municipality of Sichuan province-where party members allowed to select delegates to party congresses through secret ballots
- independent candidates allowed to stand in local elections in Beijing.

Question C8 (continued)

However

- no mass movement for political reform in China but growing evidence that Chinese citizens are prepared to challenge the authorities
- urban protests have become increasingly common but politically organised opposition is tiny
- homes of dissidents under police guard
- Chinese Democracy Movement supporters are closely watched, phones bugged and Internet access denied
- village control has been returned to party secretaries from elected village chiefs
- media must not encourage 'public intellectuals'
- Chinese Communist Party tolerates no opposition and relies on the support of the armed forces to maintain the status quo
- other relevant points.

Study Theme 3C: The United States of America

Question C9

Developed, exemplified, balanced and analytical answers may refer to:

- Affirmative Action programmes affecting minority groups in employment: Outreach, Market Advantage, Targeted Training and Investment Program
- No Child Left Behind Act
- Federal Food Stamp Program-tokens to provide needy with food
- TANF (Temporary Assistance for Needy Families)
- Head Start
- Unemployment Insurance (UI) programme (states set their own rules)
- Medicare (Federal) and Medicaid (State)
- creation of black middle class
- home ownership for Blacks at 48% in 2004-up 6% in 10 years; rate for Latinos similar
- on average, minorities suffer poorer incomes than Whites; accumulated wealth inequalities even greater than income inequalities and growing. However, some groups of Asians, Cubans and Native Americans have higher average incomes than Whites
- biggest determinant of how far you go in life in the USA is how far you go in education; huge income gap between college and non-college educated
- American education financed largely by local property taxes
- only 10% of students in most selective universities come from bottom half of the income scale
- aid to black colleges has been cut at both state and federal level
- budget squeeze on all states between 2001 and 2004 forced them to increase fees at state colleges, traditionally the places attended by the children of less wealthy parents

Question C9 (continued)

- Supreme Court ruling that 'mechanical' devices such as quotas are not allowed but race may be considered as one factor among others
- Latino teenagers are three times more likely than Whites to drop out of school and twice as likely as Blacks
- between 1975-2001 the share of America's wealth held by the poorest 20% fell from 4.4% to 3.5%. In the same period, the share held by the richest 20% increased from 43.2% to 50.1%
- Bush proposals for Social Security reform
- other relevant points.

Study Theme 3D: The European Union

Question C10

Developed, exemplified, balanced and analytical answers may refer to:
- European Parliament is 'the crucible of a supranational democracy'
- may force the Commission to resign (as it did in 1999)
- may reject the nomination of a new president for the Commission
- has the power of veto over new members and association agreements
- co-decision powers give it the right to amend and veto, but not to initiate, legislation over most of what the EU does
- once seen as only a talking shop, its powers have been expanded. Plays a vital role in shaping everything from business to the environment
- a key power is its control over the EC budget in many areas, including development cooperation
- if approved, an EU constitution would expand its co-decision powers from 39 to 80 policy areas
- reportedly has a say in 80% of the legislation passed in the EU.

   However, the Council:
- is the EU decision-maker
- discusses proposals put forward by the Commission, decides what form these proposals should take, amends them if necessary and decides whether or not they should become law
- takes many decisions behind closed doors.
- the co-decision procedure does not apply to either tax matters or foreign policy-it may only give a 'non-binding' opinion
- claim that there is no public interest or engagement in the EU Parliament-low turnout (46%) in elections
- other relevant points.

Study Theme 3E: The Politics of Development in Africa

Question C11

Developed, exemplified, balanced and analytical answers may refer to:
- alleged corruption and mismanagement
- land tenure
- debt accumulation and policies (cash crops, taxation) to finance repayments
- effects on foreign investment of unpredictable enforcement of regulations, uncertain application of laws, lack of confidence in courts and weak protection for rights of property ownership
- education and health policy issues
- war/civil war as a consequence/extension of domestic policies
- effectiveness and appropriateness of different types of foreign generated aid
- terms of trade
- extent of foreign interference in domestic politics
- debt cancellation
- natural disasters
- other relevant points.

Study Theme 3F: Global Security

Question C12

Developed, exemplified, balanced and analytical answers may refer to:
- no longer the West's cold-war armed club with eyes on the Fulda Gap
- emphasis now on specialist forces, mobility and counter-terrorism as opposed to nuclear and large scale armoured forces
- now in partnership with former potential adversaries
- still committed to the defence of democracy; now assists in establishing a democratic and prosperous Eastern Europe, and bringing Russia into the European Security system
- accepts that member states might need to participate in global peacekeeping duties in order to defend their security interests
- continue to promote stability in Europe by preventing and managing regional conflicts
- now considers requests from the UN to get involved in UN peacekeeping duties on a case by case basis, both within and without the Euro-Atlantic area
- view that having lost its focus as a defensive alliance, it has not found a role with which to replace it; it is too unwieldy to fight terrorism, and is little more than the USA's 'cleaning lady', if and when required
- Partnership for Peace preceded admission of Poland, Hungary and the Czech Republic in 1999, thus increasing membership from 16 to 19
- admitted seven more members in 2004, including the three former Soviet Republics of Estonia, Latvia and Lithuania, together with Slovenia, Slovakia, Bulgaria and Romania
- applicant countries include Macedonia, Albania, Croatia and Ukraine
- implications of increased membership
- other relevant points.

Modern Studies Higher
Specimen Paper 2 – Decision Making
Exercise 2007

1. Source A states that the percentage of elderly is projected to grow which C1 confirms. Source A also states that the percentage of working age will decline significantly which Source C1 does not confirm.

2. Edwin states that the elderly get the biggest share of government spending on benefits which C2(a) confirms. He also states that a higher percentage of families with children live on very low incomes. C2(b) shows that this is true of single parent families but not true of two parent families.

3. Patricia states that the majority of elderly people do not claim means tested benefits. Source C3 shows that a majority of pensioners do claim these benefits. Patricia also states that local authority tenants lose a smaller percentage of their income than owner occupiers though they are more likely to claim. Source C3 shows a –41·1% loss for tenants compared to –12·8% for owner occupiers but also shows that a higher percentage of tenants claim benefits.

4. *Credit will be given to:*
   - An introduction that indicates an awareness of the role to be adopted and makes a clear recommendation.
   - Developed arguments in support of the recommendation.
   - Identification of, comment on, and rebuttal of counter arguments.
   - Synthesis of the Source information.
   - Provision and use of appropriate background knowledge.
   - An overall conclusion.
   - A style appropriate to a report (sub-headings, chapters, etc).

Arguments for the proposal may feature:
   - Inconsistency of approach to benefits provision.
   - Cost of free care in Scotland and projected cost if it were made free throughout UK.
   - Need to fund other more pressing priorities.
   - Elderly already receive large % of public spending.
   - Problems over delivery of free care in Scotland.
   - Means testing is an efficient use of resources.
   - Over half of pensioners do claim means tested benefits.

Question 4. (continued)

Arguments against the proposal may feature:
   - Elderly expect/deserve help from the Welfare State.
   - Increased take up rate indicates a real need for free care.
   - Evidence of Sutherland report-unrealistic to separate personal from medical care which is free at the point of use.
   - Significant numbers of old people do not claim means tested benefits; effects on pensioners' incomes.
   - Discourages saving.
   - Problems over means testing in England.
   - Possible use of extra 3p/£ income tax under devolution.

Other points may include
   - Possible conflict with the original aims of the Welfare State.
   - Reference to other priorities within the NHS and Social Services.
   - Differences between and within political parties, eg Blairite Labour in England and more traditional Labour in Scotland.
   - Demographic 'time bomb' and its effects.
   - Further development of the Sutherland report.
   - Political importance of the elderly-the 'grey vote'.
   - Case studies of the elderly and their problems.
   - Media reports.
   - Personal experience.
   - Other valid points.

Modern Studies Higher
Paper 1 – 2007

Section A – Political Issues in the United Kingdom

Study Theme 1A – Devolved Decision Making in Scotland

Question A1

"Pass" and better answers should feature developed, exemplified knowledge and understanding of:
The reserved and devolved powers
Decisions arising from these made in Westminster and Holyrood respectively
and
Balanced comment on/analysis of the perceived "importance" of these decisions for Scotland.
Answers may refer to:

- reserved powers include constitutional issues, defence, foreign policy, treasury matters and social security
- Westminster decides on the level of the Scottish Parliament's budget
- any revision of the Scotland Act must be passed by Westminster
- the 'Sewel Motion' procedure gives Westminster the power to legislate in an area supposedly devolved to Holyrood
- the range of devolved powers includes education, environment, health, justice and transport
- the Scottish Parliament has limited powers of taxation – it can vary (upwards or downwards) the rate of income tax by 3p in the £; it can vary the business rate – but has no fiscal autonomy
- laws passed by the Scottish Parliament include free personal care for the elderly; free nursery places for 3/4 year olds, free bus travel for pensioners, the abolition of tuition fees, a new voting system for local government, abolition of smoking in public places. Candidates may comment on the importance of these (and others)
- responsibility for agriculture and fisheries is devolved but the Scottish Parliament can only contribute as part of a UK delegation
- the Scottish Parliament cannot deal directly with Europe on issues such as crime, health and the environment, all of which are devolved
- the Home Office has rejected calls for tougher gun laws and limited the scope of the Fresh Talent Initiative
- despite a widely supported campaign north of the border, the Scottish Parliament could not prevent the amalgamation of the Scottish regiments
- Scotland not allowed a separate protocol on the forced removal of failed asylum seekers

Question A1 (continued)

- Westminster can decide how many nuclear power stations should be built but the Scottish Parliament decides on whether or not to award planning permission
- survey results have indicated that only 23% think that the Executive has most influence over how Scotland is run. A majority of voters see the reserved issues as the more important.
- in 2005, Jack McConnell wanted to review the responsibility for making laws on firearms restrictions, drugs, nuclear power stations, casinos, abortion, certain benefits, broadcasting and immigration – he was, reportedly, ordered to halt his "mission-creep" by Westminster
- in a YouGov poll (December 2006) 62% wanted the Scottish Parliament to have more powers
- other relevant points and issues.

Study Theme 1B – Decision Making in Central Government

Question A2

"Pass" and better answers should feature developed, exemplified knowledge and understanding of:
The powers of the Prime Minister
The opportunities afforded Parliament (Commons & Lords) to exercise control over these powers
and
Balanced comment on/analysis of the extent to which Parliament can control the powers of the Prime Minister.
Answers may refer to:

- powers of the Prime Minister derived from being party leader with the gift of patronage, leader of Her Majesty's Government, in charge of the Prime Minister's office, the leading UK representative on the world stage, the general election date decider, the Parliamentary link with the monarch.
- control traditionally seen as being exercised in both the Commons through debates, Prime Minister's Question Time, early day motions, select committees, inquiries, the Liaison Committee, the possibility of a no confidence motion, back bench revolts and in the House of Lords (in which at present, the Government does not have a majority)
- the Lib-Dems claim that the Salisbury Convention (do not oppose bills on which the winners campaigned) no longer stands
- claim that Parliament has seldom been more assertive than in recent years given the number of revolts in the Commons and the increase in the number of Government defeats in the Lords since the removal of most hereditary peers in 1999

Modern Studies Higher
Paper 1 – 2007 (cont.)

Question A2 (continued)

- before 2001, Labour MPs accused of using Prime Minister's Question Time as a cringe-making competition in sycophancy. This changed in July 2001 when the Commons forced the Government to re-instate the chairs of each of the Foreign Affairs and Transport Select committees. In each vote over 100 Labour MPs voted against their own party
- over top-up fees, the Prevention of Terrorism Bill and the Religious Hatred Bill, the Government gave way on legislation in order to ensure its passage through the Commons
- Tony Blair did respond to the Butler Report's observation of his informal style of decision making by promising to curb his 'government by sofa'
- parliamentary control limited by the executive's control of the parliamentary timetable, the whip system, the payroll vote and the presidential nature of the Prime Minister's office
- Tony Blair's first ever defeat in the Commons was in November 2005 on the proposal to allow the detention of suspected terrorists for 90 days
- the rebellions over Iraq – the largest saw 139 Labour MPs defy the whip (2003) – were the largest on any policy since modern British party politics began
- two defeats during passage of the Racial and Religious Hatred Bill were as a result of a failure in whipping.
- the Prime Minister has better jobs to offer than the leader of the opposition, and has all the weight and expertise of the civil service to provide ministers with clever answers to awkward questions and can usually rely upon a healthy majority
- view that the only checks on the Prime Minister's power of patronage are informal – often through opinions voiced in the media (e.g. the coming to light in November 2005 of Tony Blair's proposals to award contributors to the political funds of the Labour and Conservative parties)
- parliament's role is to scrutinise not control
- other relevant points and issues.

Study Theme 1C – Political Parties and their Policies (including the Scottish Dimension)

Question A3

Assess the importance of party unity in achieving electoral success.
"Pass" and better answers should feature developed, exemplified knowledge and understanding of:
The importance of party unity to electoral success
Other factors that may enhance/damage electoral success
and
Balanced comment on/analysis of the importance of party unity in achieving electoral success.

Answers may refer to:

- with less electoral party loyalty than in the past, a united election campaign regarded as important to achieving electoral success
- damage was done to the Conservative Party by its obsession with Europe and its leadership wrangles
- electoral successes of 'new' (united) Labour
- link between 'quality' of leadership and perceived party unity, and its impact on polling indicators of electoral support
- impact of Cameron on support for the Conservative Party
- rivalries between 'old Labour' and the 'Blairites' and between Brown and Blair claimed to have been one explanation of Labour's poorer showing in 2005
- continued disagreement between 'fundamentalists' and 'gradualists' is said to have undermined electoral support for the SNP in the 2003 Scottish Parliament election in which SNP lost 8 MSPs, and its share of the vote fell to less than 20%
- disagreement evident in SNP leadership/ deputy leadership elections said to have damaged the party; 2005 General Election popular vote share was lowest since 1987, but did increase the number of MPs from 4 to 6 (the Salmond Bounce?)
- continued sniping at the quality of Charles Kennedy's leadership of the Liberal Democrats culminated in his resignation
- membership base (the Conservative Party membership has fallen from a peak of over 2 million to less than 250,000) and financial position. (Conservative Party reportedly clear of its £16m debt, January 2007, whilst Labour in debt to tune of £23m)
- the winning habit (importance of local elections)
- party policies on key issues
- the media and voters (ST 1C descriptor)

Question A3 (continued)

- the electoral system (AMS) in Scotland (appears in neither ST 1C Descriptor nor Coverage, but candidates may transfer KU from either ST 1A or ST 1D)
- view that parties have become more united in recent years as party policies have become less 'ideological' and differences between the main parties less ideological too
- other relevant points and issues.

Study Theme 1D – Electoral Systems, Voting and Political Attitudes

Question A4

"Pass" and better answers should feature developed, exemplified knowledge and understanding of:
The main voter "choice" and "representation" features of the AMS
The main voter "choice" and "representation" features of FPTP
and
Balanced comment on/analysis of whether the AMS or FPTP gives voters more choice and better representation.
Top marks may be achieved without reference to the 2007 Scottish Parliamentary election.
Answers may refer to:
AMS
- voters have two votes: constituency and list
- there are no wasted votes
- degree of proportionality allows for wider range of parties featuring in the Scottish Parliament
- list can be used to increase minority representation and facilitate gender balance
- result likely to encourage consensus rather than conflict politics on the part of the elected, thus broadening voter representation at the highest decision-making level
- a greater proportion of voters likely to get a policy implemented that they voted for
- gives voters a range of representatives (8 in Scotland) from different parties to discuss an issue with
FPTP
- effective choice limited to marginal seats
- no proportionality
- wasted votes
- a large proportion of voters get neither an MP, nor the Government, nor the policy implementation that they voted for
- said to produce elected dictatorships; in 2005 Labour got 55% of the seats with 36% of the votes – the lowest winning party vote share in history
- in both systems the voter has little say in the selection of candidates
- in AMS closed party lists restricts voter choice as the parties need not name their candidates

Question A4 (continued)

- AMS still retains the so-called negative features of the constituency vote and is not wholly proportional, but more so than FPTP; in 2003 Labour polled 32% of the vote for its 38% seats
- There are no by-elections in AMS so voters denied 'protest-vote' opportunities or any say in who their new representative should be
- AMS produces coalitions and compromise policies that no one voted for
- AMS produces disproportional representation in the Executive; the Liberal Democrats were the fourth most popular party with 13% of the vote (in 2003)
- the proportion of minority ethnic MPs is higher under FPTP in the House of Commons
- 33.3% of the Scottish Parliament is female; for Westminster the figure is 18%
- "backdoor entry" to Parliament via the list may result in MSPs and even members of the Executive, for whom no one voted
- the role of the regional/list members is obscure. To whom are they accountable?
- arguably little evidence of consensus
- Issues arising from the 2007 Scottish Parliamentary Election
- other relevant points and issues.

Section B – Social Issues in the United Kingdom

Study Theme 2 – Wealth and Health Inequalities in the United Kingdom

Question B5

"Pass" and better answers should feature developed, exemplified knowledge and understanding of:
The founding principles of the Welfare State
Government Welfare State/State welfare policies
and
Balanced comment on/analysis of the extent to which Government policies enable the founding principles of the Welfare State to be met.
Answers may refer to:
- solution to the problems of want, disease, ignorance, squalor and idleness seen in the "traditional" collectivist approach
- benefits to provide social security to protect the population from cradle to the grave.
Income
- range of Government benefits available for those out of work, including Income Support and Jobseekers Allowance, becoming increasingly means tested
- the National Minimum Wage
- issue of paying for pensions
- launch of campaign against child poverty in 1999, child poverty in Scotland reduced by 25% (target) in 2005 (for UK by 23%)
Health
- evidence of inequalities between social classes and gender/race

Modern Studies Higher
Paper 1 – 2007 (cont.)

Question B5 (continued)

- New Labour's "holistic" approach to health care; good-health promotion campaigns, bans on smoking; PPP; welfare to work strategies aims to improve the quality of life
- Government still provides care but asks individuals to take responsibility too
- issue of charges.

Education
- recent public and privately channelled investment in education
- issue of fees/loans for higher education
- SureStart

Housing
- lack of available council housing
- impact of boom in property prices on first-time buyers
- role of housing associations
- housing benefit

Employment
- the welfare to work (a hand up, not a hand out) strategy
- Tax Credits
- New Deals
- Pathways to Work
- SureStart
- the idea of universalism has faced substantial pressure in the past few years
- instead of universal benefits that are largely flat rate, the expansion of means-testing, ('targeting') has led to the creation of benefits like Pension Credit and also tax credits
- Tax Credits are near universal benefits directed at all but the richest 10% of families with children
- proposals for incapacity benefit reform
- contributory principle under threat
- the idea of a state monopoly has been tempered to some degree by greater involvement of the private and voluntary sectors
- UK has one of the highest child poverty rates in developed countries
- labour market polarised between work-rich and work-poor households
- financial support for working parents is now amongst the most generous for low-paid employees in the OECD
- no set targets for reducing poverty in the population as a whole; work may reduce the risk of poverty but it does not eliminate it
- Government policy has been most successful in dealing with "blockbuster" poverty – the poverty suffered by the greatest number of people – by giving the poor more money
- Government would insist that changes are in keeping with the concept of 'modern' collectivism
- other relevant points and issues.

Question B6
"Pass" and better answers should feature developed, exemplified knowledge and understanding of:
Inequalities in the UK
Government policies to reduce these inequalities and/or reasons for these inequalities
and
Balanced comment on/analysis of the extent to which inequalities continue to exist in the UK.
Answers may refer to:
Social and Economic Inequalities linked to age, gender, race, social class, region;

- huge inequalities in the way that care and support are made available to older people
- continued evidence of "glass ceiling" (might be cracked, not yet broken). New "glass partition" – women concentrating in the less well-paid sectors of the professions
- women still earning less than men in part-time and full-time jobs; men in full-time employment now earning 18% more an hour than women
- extent of racism
- ethnic minorities find it difficult to get jobs; and many are more likely to be unemployed than white males of the same age and level of education
- the social class wealth and health gap
- claim that the "disadvantaged dying" become part of the "revolving door" system; labelled as "bed blockers" as if being ill and not getting treatment were their own fault
- North-South wealth and health divide
- gap in living standards between the well paid and those on benefits
- lone-parent families
- continued existence of poverty: view that the UK's most troubled group, in both absolute and relative terms, is poor, white and British born
- expansion of the middle class has made it harder than ever for the working classes to get better high-earning professional jobs
- all groups have become more prosperous but the gap between the classes has not narrowed
- North-South split widening; difference within regions; Glasgow labelled "a swamp of poverty" because all ten of the most deprived areas in Scotland are in the city (Scottish Index of Multiple Deprivation); Northern areas of England have higher obesity rates, more smoking related deaths and lower life expectancies than Southern areas
- view that gender equality is no longer a live issue – girls are high achievers at school; high % of women MSPs; Solicitor General is a woman; opening up of medicine, the legal profession and the church (where there is an increasing demand for part-time clergy) to women
- General Household Survey analysis shows that UK born ethnic minorities seem to be doing the same jobs as similarly qualified whites and earning similar amounts

Question B6 (continued)

- children of Afro-Caribbean and Indian immigrants have closed the earnings gap with whites in both professional and blue-collar work
- other relevant points

Government/local policies/strategies to reduce inequalities:

- candidates may select from a wide range of these and should demonstrate a link with the "wealth/health inequalities" features in their answer
- promise to end child poverty forever
- gender and race legislation
- Equalities Act (2006) _ under the Act the Commission for and Human Rights (CEHR) will bring together the Disability Rights Commission and the Equal Opportunities Commission from October 2007. The Commission for Racial Equality will join in 2009, putting expertise on equality, diversity and human rights all in one place
- other relevant points and issues.

Section C – International Issues

Study Theme 3A – The Republic of South Africa

Question C7

"Pass" and better answers should feature developed, exemplified knowledge and understanding of:
The democratic features of the South African political system
The part played by the ANC and other political groups in the South African political system
and
Balanced comment on/analysis of the suggestion that South Africa has become a one party state.

Answers may refer to:

- South Africa is a constitutional democracy with a three tier system of government and an independent judiciary
- Party List Electoral system
- 16 parties represented in parliament
- 97 parties contested the 2006 elections
- President, elected by the National Assembly, is permitted to serve a maximum of two five-year terms (but nothing, technically, to prevent someone serving a third term as president of the ANC)
- written Constitution and Constitutional Court
- Constitutional (Bill of Rights) guarantees include property rights and education
- free press and a robust legal system
- recognition of trade unionism
- ANC has a huge majority in the National Assembly and is the dominant party in the provinces
- there are 6 non-black "co-opted" cabinet members
- ANC has not tampered with the Constitution and accepted decisions of the Constitutional court

Question C7 (continued)

- no concept of a "loyal opposition"; the Democratic Alliance Party, the second largest in the National Assembly has 50 seats (ANC has 285) out of 400
- ANC said to dismiss ideas from outside its own bureaucracy (e.g. response to the HIV/AIDS crisis) and to meet any criticism with accusations of racism
- claims by Desmond Tutu of the emergence of a culture of "sycophantic obsequious conformity"
- some SABC commentators blacklisted in 2006 for being too critical of the Government; judges and journalists are told to "work together to build the nation"
- Inkatha Freedom Party claims that the ANC is determined to alter or remove the legislative authority of the provinces and warns against the danger of South Africa becoming a one party state
- COSATU plays little part in economic policy decisions
- Jacob Zuma on record as claiming that the ANC will remain in office "until Jesus comes back"
- ANC remains extremely popular; its vote share has risen in each of three elections (1994/1999/2004) due to a combination of factors: the struggle to end apartheid and bring democracy/its record in office/the opposition parties are so weak
- other relevant points and issues.

Study Theme 3B – The People's Republic of China

Question C8

"Pass" and better answers should feature developed, exemplified knowledge and understanding of:
Recent social and economic reform policies of the Chinese Government
The impact of these reforms on Chinese society
and
Balanced comment on/analysis of the overall effects of social and economic reform.

Answers may refer to:

- relaxation of the hukuo – urban/rural classification of population
- dismantling of the danwei – work unit behaviour control organisation
- relaxation in rural areas of One Child Policy
- reduction in waiting time for those who qualify to have a second child
- better rights for women
- development of private education and health services
- right to own property now written into the Constitution
- encouragement of foreign investment
- promotion of capitalist ideas – introduction of easier credit for business, support for entrepreneurs

Modern Studies Higher
Paper 1 – 2007 (cont.)

Question C8 (continued)

- increase in subsidies and greater investment in agriculture
- tax reform
- "great development of the west" policy to boost development in western regions
- awarding of the "dragonhead status" to favoured districts
- gradual changes to the judicial system: increased legal representation
- huge and sustained rises in economic growth
- incomes have risen in the cities, particularly in the coastal areas
- mining held up as an example of the success of policy to invest in the west of China
- claim that the number of poor has fallen sharply in recent years
- greater social freedoms
- expanding wealthy middle class and greatly improved standard of living
- paper recycling tycoon Zhang Yin became the first woman to top China's rich list in October 2006
- uneven rise in farm income
- as a result of tax reform and subsidies, rural incomes have increased but urban incomes have grown much faster
- huge urban/rural and employed/unemployed income/lifestyle inequalities
- homelessness and overcrowding in the large cities exacerbated by migration
- poor working conditions in many factories
- allegations of corruption on the part of local CPC officials in managing change
- the UN Development Programme claims that 50 million farmers have been thrown off the land with little or no compensation
- 20-30 million State Owned Enterprise workers have lost their jobs
- widespread and sustained rural protest: 87,000 "contradictions within the people" recorded in 2005
- problems associated with pollution
- other relevant points and issues.

Study Theme 3C – The United States of America

Question C9

"Pass" and better answers should feature developed, exemplified knowledge and understanding of:

Ethnic minority participation in elections in the USA

The importance of the minority ethnic vote/ethnic minority issues to the outcome of elections in the USA

and

Balanced comment on/analysis of the extent to which ethnic minorities influence the outcome of elections in the USA.

Answers may refer to:

- minorities make up 30% of the US population and their population share is growing, with Hispanics being the fastest growing
- minority groups less likely to either register or vote than Whites; only African Americans have registration and turnout in excess of 50%
- registration of APIs and Hispanics is less than 40% and turnout fails to reach 30%
- for Whites registration is almost 68% and turnout just above 60%
- concentration on ethnic minority voters in key 'swing states' of California, Texas, New York and Florida gives them disproportionate influence in the presidential elections
- growing potential impact of the Hispanic vote in Arizona, Colorado, Nevada and New Mexico
- traditionally the ethnic minority vote has gone to the Democratic Party; although a majority for Kerry in 2004, Bush still won the presidential elections
- importance of the ethnic minority vote recognised in the composition of the Bush Cabinet
- Blacks are most solid in their support of the Democrats (90%); for Hispanics the level of support is 55% and for APIs, 59%
- Democrats use a variety of methods to get out the minority vote. Republicans more likely to be accused of using "dirty tricks" to prevent black voters getting to the polls
- most of the Black Democrats in Congress come from majority Black districts
- at local levels, electoral success may depend upon involvement of ethnic minority voters in a coalition with Whites; Antonio R Villariagosa, LA's first Latino mayor since 1872 was elected in 2005, with 59% of the vote by forging a coalition that included Black voters as well as Latinos and Whites
- nine Indian Americans were winners in the November 2006 US elections to national, state and local offices including Minnesota State Senator Chaudhary (Democrat) whose constituency is largely White

Question C9 (continued)

- view that Hispanic voters, annoyed by the Republican hard line on immigration, turned out in force, and helped the Democrats win the November 2006 congressional elections
- both Hillary Clinton and Barrack Obama courting the minority vote in their presidential candidate campaigns
- thanks to gerrymandering and the ease with which those in power can raise money, usually 90% of those who run for the House of Representatives tend to be re-elected
- importance of gender (women have tended to be more significantly supportive of the Democrat candidate than men); religion (Protestants more pro-Republican and Catholics more pro-Democrat) and the "religious right"; the 'wealth gap' – not as influential as it was; geographic region, with the Northeast having become the new heartland of the Democratic Party and the Republicans now in control of the socially conservative South
- in congressional (and presidential) elections the big issues are at present terrorism, the war in Iraq, the economy and jobs and moral issues. However, an alleged racial slur said to have cost the incumbent George Allen (Virginia) his seat in the Senate, losing to the Democrat James Webb by 0.3% of the vote
- other relevant points and issues.

Study Theme 3D – The European Union

Question C10

"Pass" and better answers should feature developed, exemplified knowledge and understanding of:
The main agreed social and economic policies of the EU
Issues on which there is disagreement amongst the current membership
and
Balanced comment on/analysis of the extent to which there is agreement on social and economic policies in the EU.

Answers may refer to:

Agreed aims of:
- regional policy
- social policies
- common agricultural policy
- fisheries policy
- economic policy.

Disagreement "issues":
- criteria for regional aid
- the working time directive
- response to UK proposal on a prison transfer scheme
- reform of CAP and the UK rebate issue
- response to the ETS (emissions trading scheme)
- fish stock protection measures and quotas: allegations that some national enforcement agencies are less efficient than others; resistance to reform by entrenched interests in Spain, France, Portugal and Greece
- single currency

Question C10 (continued)

- single market; consequences of economic migration
- the budget
- further enlargement
- an EU constitution
- foreign policy
- rules for accepting workers from Eastern Europe
- other relevant points and issues.

Study Theme 3E – The Politics of Development in Africa

Question C11

"Pass" and better answers should feature developed, Specific African countries exemplified, knowledge and understanding of:
The contribution of sources/forms of foreign aid to the development needs of African countries
Factors that may limit the impact of foreign aid on development
and
Balanced comment on/analysis of the suggestion that foreign aid alone is no guarantee of development.

Answers may refer to:
- sources of foreign aid: international; governmental; non-governmental; the forms they take (grants, donations, loans, advice, short and long-term projects, food aid etc) and their contribution to development
- the Millennium Development Goals: eradication of extreme poverty and hunger; achievement of universal primary education; promotion of gender equality and empowerment of women; reduction in child mortality; improvement in maternal health; combating HIV/AIDS, malaria and other diseases; environmental sustainability; global partnership for development
- misuse of aid – not only confined to military spending by those in authority. In Nigeria, bed nets for protection against the mosquito were made into wedding gowns
- money does not always go where it is intended
- consequences of civil and international strife
- questions over the relevance of some aid: many threats to public health do not need hospitals, highly trained clinicians or expensive medical treatment. On the other hand there is no good in handing out AIDS drugs without the infrastructure to back them up – major investment in nurses, hospitals, sanitation and utilities
- terms of trade policies of the developed world
- view that DOHA did not deliver because of the trade policies of poor countries. 50% of what developing countries would gain from fully free trade would come from their own tariff cuts because 1/3 of their exports are to other poor countries and their tariffs are much higher (many relying on tariffs as a source of revenue)

Modern Studies Higher
Paper 1 – 2007 (cont.)

Question C11 (continued)

- view that trade liberalisation is no substitution for either domestic reform or foreign aid
- view that if Africa increased its share of world trade by just 1%, it would bring an extra £34b per annum (five times what it receives in aid). Freer trade would cut the number of Sub-Saharan Africans in absolute poverty by 60 million
- "aid without trade is a lullaby – a song you sing to children to get them to sleep" (Yoweri Musevini)
- selective approach of Heavily Indebted Poor Countries Initiative – debts of Somalia and Sudan have not been dropped
- view that wiping out debt acts as a disincentive to those trying to become financially stable and rewards those that do not
- problems of so-called "failed states" whose people suffer from "bad governance"
- NEPAD has accepted that in order to secure foreign aid, African governments must reform and be more transparent in their use of aid from Developed Nations
- claims that aid causes corruption, creates dependency and discourages entrepreneurship
- view that addressing infrastructure impediments is the most effective way to stimulate poverty reduction and economic growth
- even when aid is "properly" used, development does not come overnight; when Zambia's foreign debt was reduced, most of the savings spent on recruiting teachers and improving health care (fees for basic health care removed). Nevertheless, Zambia remains poor and still depends on aid
- recognition by both the UN Investing in Development: A Practical Plan to achieve the Millennium Goals and the Commission for Africa that "more aid is needed to meet Africa's development needs". However "outsiders cannot deliver development, it must be done by Africans" (Commission for Africa report)
- Millennium Project has set up 12 "research villages" (target of 1000 by 2009) in 10 African countries to pioneer models of development (The Magnificent Seven) that can be copied but there is an admission that successful implementation depends upon foreign aid
- other relevant points and issues

Study Theme 3F – Global Security

Question C12

"Pass" and better answers should feature developed, exemplified knowledge and understanding of:
Threats to global security
Sources (candidates may select from UN, NATO, AU, EU, USA and coalition allies) and forms of international responses to threats to global security
and
Balanced comment on/analysis of the effectiveness of international responses to threats to global security.

Answers may refer to:
Threats:
- civil conflict
- international disputes
- nuclear proliferation
- post-conflict recovery (peace building)
- terrorism
- unstable regimes

Responses:
- UN – Democratic Republic of the Congo, Eritrea, Lebanon, Ethiopia, Sudan; response to acquisition of nuclear weapons by North Korea
- NATO – Bosnia, Macedonia, Kosovo, Afghanistan (where in October 2006 it took charge of Afghanistan's eastern provinces, which had been under the control of US forces since Taliban ousted in 2001)
- African Union – Sudan (forces airlifted there by EU and NATO)
- EU – Bosnia, where EUFOR took over control of peacekeeping operations from NATO in February 2005 (80% of the force simply changed badges); diplomatic response to Iran's nuclear ambitions
- USA (and coalition allies) – Iraq and The War on Terrorism
- 2005 Rand Corporation study of American and UN peacekeeping operations concluded that UN missions were not only cheaper, but had higher success rate and enjoyed greater international legitimacy
- Canadian study attributed the dramatic decline in the number of conflicts in the past decade to the "huge increase" in preventative diplomacy and peacekeeping "for the most part authorised and mounted by the UN"
- for most of the UN's history the powerful have by-passed the Security Council when they chose to
- UN is hampered by its Charter, veto, and modus operandi: fact finding mission > Security Council approval > need to find peacekeepers
- UN resolutions ignored by members
- sanction breaking
- AU initially turned down offer of UN help in Darfur

Question C12 (continued)

- initial refusal of Sudanese government to allow UN intervention in Darfur, accusing the UN of being an agent of the West. However, it agreed to allow in a "hybrid" UN and AU force
- Sudan has the backing of China and Russia who consistently water-down attempts to impose sanctions
- UN resolution 1718 (October 2006) belatedly imposed sanctions on North Korea (China had hitherto blocked) but included no reference to military intervention as USA had proposed
- USA lobby to put an American in charge of all UN peacekeeping operations seen as a move that could offer Washington an exit strategy in Iraq. (USA contributes 0.5% of UN peacekeepers)
- despite its headline failures, the scandalous behaviour of some corrupt officials and the unacceptable behaviour of some of its peacekeepers, the UN is still regarded as an essential organisation for achieving a better, fairer, more peaceful world
- view that the UN Secretary General (Ban Ki-moon) cannot succeed without Washington's co-operation and reform of the organisation
- election held in the DR (Democratic Republic) Congo (2006)
- EU unable to agree over either war in Iraq (2001-2003) or Israel's war in Lebanon
- difficulties facing NATO in defeating the Taliban militarily
- USA-British difficulties in Iraq
- other relevant points and issues.

Modern Studies Higher
Paper 2 – Decision Making Exercise 2007

1. Russell Barclay claims (Source A) that "long-term sickness and disability is the most common reason given by both men and women for not working". Source C1 shows this to be true of men but not of women.

2. (a) Russell Barclay claims (Source A) that "the UK already spends a greater percentage of its GDP on schemes for disabled workers than any other country in the EU".
   Source C2(a) shows that the UK spends less than most of the other EU countries listed.

   (b) Irene Graham claims (Source B) that charities already "spend more on the disabled than on any other group".
   Source C2(b) shows that more is spent on children.

3. Irene Graham claims (Source B) that "UK Government spending on the sick and disabled is already lower than for any other group and a lower percentage of one-parent families receive Incapacity/Disability Benefit than any other benefit".
   Source C3(a) shows spending on (any one of) three other groups to be lower.
   Source C3(b) shows that, for the benefits listed, 9% (by far the lowest) of one-parent families receive Incapacity/Disability Benefit.

4. Credit will be given to:
   A style appropriate to a report (sub-headings, chapters etc) with:
   - an introduction that indicates an awareness of the role to be adopted and makes a clear recommendation
   - developed arguments in support of the recommendation
   - identification of and comment on (rebuttal of) counter arguments
   - synthesis of source information
   - provision and use of appropriate background knowledge
   - an overall conclusion.
   Arguments for the proposal may feature:
   - increased spending must be brought under control
   - evidence that not all claimants are incapable of work
   - proposal maintains original aims of the welfare state in encouraging work/discouraging idleness
   - work is now less physically demanding
   - work is beneficial to the individual
   - provision of useful training for those who can work
   - genuine claimants will be better off

Modern Studies Higher
Paper 2 – Decision Making Exercise 2007 (cont.)

Question 4. (continued)

- existing recipients of IB not affected.

Arguments against the proposal may feature:
- reduction in number of claimants already happening as the existing system is already a tough one
- charities have to underpin an under-funded welfare state
- increased stress on vulnerable individuals
- concern of experts over implications
- priority should be to overcome employer prejudice
- UK spends less on helping disabled workers than most EU states
- original aims of the welfare state being compromised
- yet another money saving device.

Credit will be given to background knowledge, developed from source material references to:

Source A
- We are encouraging welfare dependency at the expense of individual responsibility (lines 12/13).
- ...and give the taxpayer better value for their money (line 15).
- We are determined to continue to move people from welfare into work (lines 24/25).
- ...the fundamental principles of the welfare state (lines 29/30).

Source B
- ...the cost of the welfare state (line 9).
- ...other groups vulnerable to poverty, such as lone-parents (line 17).
- "Welfare to Work" policies (lines 18/19).
- Effective laws to prevent discrimination against the disabled (line 25).
- ...social exclusion and...the collectivist principles of the welfare state (lines 29/30).

Other background knowledge-based arguments may include:
- the long-term increase in the cost of social welfare which was not anticipated by Beveridge (infinite demand for finite resources)
- whether or not the proposal is in conflict with the original aims of the welfare state
- the extent and causes of poverty in the UK political debate: Labour back-bench revolt over IB reform; policy differences between Blairites and traditional Labour
- foreign comparisons
- recent media coverage
- other relevant issues/points.

Modern Studies Higher
Paper 1 – 2008

SECTION A - Political Issues in the United Kingdom

Study Theme 1A: Devolved Decision Making in Scotland

Question A1

"Pass" and better answers should feature developed, exemplified knowledge and understanding of:
- The part played by local government (responsibilities and decision making powers) in a devolved Scotland
- The limitations on local government decision making powers and responsibilities in a devolved Scotland

and
- Balanced comment on/analysis of the role of local government in decision making in a devolved Scotland.

Answers may refer to:
- local government serves, represents and is accountable to, the people of different communities.
- delivery of cost-effective local services (mandatory, permissive, discretionary): importance of these.
- *Public Attitudes to Local Government in Scotland* report highlighted that throughout the UK the institution of local government is not well thought of. Generally perceived to be bureaucratic, inefficient and wasteful of public money.
- services more highly regarded than the institution.
- 38% (2005 Scottish Household Survey) agreed that their council was addressing the key issues affecting the quality of life in their neighbourhood.
- one of the principles of local government is 'inclusion for all', hence, recent injection of cash into modernising facilities and getting young people involved in physical activity.
- setting and collection of the Council Tax; 'concordat' between SNP led administration and COSLA to freeze council tax until 2010; less ring fencing of grants; councils may retain any efficiency savings they make.
- Scottish Government works in partnership with local authorities in making decisions and delivering services.
- local government issues can now be fully aired and debated in the Scottish Parliament and its committees.
- councils have better access to ministers and civil servants than previously.
- three year funding has given councils the chance to plan ahead and have brought greater financial stability.

Question A1. (continued)

- changes to Scottish Enterprise involve the transfer of 'local' responsibilities to local authorities. The responsibility for providing local business support to be handed to local councils. Move recognises the role of local authorities as players in economic development.
- Scottish Government is the top tier of government vested with the powers to legislate on local government and on Scottish domestic functions.
- majority of local government income derived from Rate Support Grant and other Scottish Government monies; weighting of grants dependent on need/ability of councils to raise Council Tax/non domestic rates.
- councils increasingly forced to implement policies they do not support, for example, PFI/PPP, 'Best Value'; concerns over funding of Free Personal Care.
- reduction in council role: social housing provided through housing stock transfers.
- council planning decisions can be, and are, overturned by the Scottish Government; Donald Trump Golf Resort issue has raised questions about the role of local government in big development projects and effectiveness of planning procedures.
- claim that local government's share of public spending has fallen to an all-time low, whilst that of unelected and unaccountable 'quangos' have risen; this is seen as an affront to local democracy.
- claim that devolution has undermined the status of local government. Pre-devolution, local government got greater media coverage. Full-time, all Scotland local government correspondents no longer exist as press attention and resources now focused on Parliament.
- implications of SNP's first budget 2007. Promised not to cut the number of councils. Withdrew previous threats of penalties for overspending. Extra funding - not ring-fenced. Seen as giving COSLA greater flexibility and responsibility.
- other relevant points.

Study Theme 1B: Decision Making in Central Government

Question A2

"Pass" and better answers should feature developed, exemplified knowledge and understanding of:

- The ways in which pressure groups attempt to influence decision making in Central Government
- The impact (successes/failures) of pressure groups on decision making in Central Government

and

- Balanced comment on/analysis of the effectiveness of pressure groups in influencing decision making in Central Government.

Answers may refer to:

- campaigns, protests, demonstrations, use of media, lobbying, petitions, e-petitions, letter writing, direct action, sponsorship of political candidates, etc.
- sectional/interest groups and promotional/cause groups.
- insider/outsider groups.
- both the number and range of pressure groups have increased in recent years; growth of single-issue groups.
- under Labour the number of sources of political power has increased and there are more decision-makers for groups to try to influence; the implementation of devolution has created new power hubs for pressure groups to focus on.
- importance of access to Government and compatibility with Government thinking; size and type of membership, funds, and tactics; prevailing social/economic/political climate; level of public support.
- a pressure group might be part of the relevant policy community on some issues but excluded on others; in the Foot and Mouth epidemic of 2001, the NFU prevented an inoculation programme but the earlier fuel protests were in part created by the fact that many smaller farmers felt they were being ignored by the government.
- despite student protest marches against proposed top-up fees, the government went ahead with proposals.
- refusal of government to introduce PR for Parliamentary elections signified the limited influence of Charter 88.
- CBI seen as clear winners; CND as clear losers. In recent years there have been more 'smaller' winners; fewer 'larger' winners.
- successful 2005 Jamie Oliver initiative to persuade the government to allocate bigger subsidies to school meals.
- failure of the Stop the War (mobilised greater numbers on the streets than Make Poverty History) and the Countryside Alliance campaigns.
- Make Poverty History campaign seen (in hindsight) as a qualified success.
- declining influence of traditional campaigning has led to pressure groups contesting elections.

Modern Studies Higher
Paper 1 – 2008 (cont.)

Question A2. (continued)

- success not always measured simply in policy outcome terms, rather the extent of engagement of the political establishment.
- so far, although there are lots of e-petitions on Number 10's website, they have mostly just allowed the disgruntled to let off steam.
- other relevant points.

STUDY THEME 1C: POLITICAL PARTIES AND THEIR POLICIES (INCLUDING THE SCOTTISH DIMENSION)

Question A3

"Pass" and better answers should feature developed, exemplified knowledge and understanding of:
- Political party policies selected from the following: law and order; taxation; education; Europe
- Differences and similarities between these policies
and
- Balanced comment on/analysis of the assertion that there are few policy differences between the main political parties.

Answers may refer to:
- Law and Order
  (Westminster 2005)
  - **Labour**: dedicated policing teams for every area; 25,000 community support officers; 1,300 more prison places; double the cash for drug treatment.
  - **Conservative**: 40,000 extra police; 10-fold rise in drug rehab places; addicts to choose rehab or prison; end some early releases; 20,000 more prison places; judges to set minimum and maximum sentences.
  - **Liberal Democrat**: 10,000 extra police; tackle drug dealers rather than cannabis users; out-of-hours school courses against 'yob' culture; local communities to decide sentences for low-level criminals.

  (Holyrood 2007)
  - **Labour**: retain DNA and fingerprints of all crime suspects; justice centres to allow criminals to carry out 'pay back' duties in communities.
  - **Conservative**: more police officers; additional investment in drug rehab services; judges to be given discretion to refuse bail/review operation of bail.
  - **Liberal Democrat**: more police; tougher community services with offenders working to repay crimes; youth justice boards.
  - **SNP**: extra police; end short term jail sentences; more info for communities on dangerous paedophiles in their area.

Question A3. (continued)
- Education
  (Westminster 2005)
  - **Labour**: parents can select specialist schools; 200 new City Academies; new powers to control truancy and disruption; university top-up fees up to £3,000, with grants for poorest students.
  - **Conservative**: 600,000 new school places to boost choice; allow good schools to expand and create new ones; heads able to expel disruptive pupils; no student fees - charge interest on loans.
  - **Liberal Democrat**: cut class sizes for youngest children; all children to be taught by a qualified teacher in each subject; abolish "unnecessary tests"; scrap university fees.

  (Holyrood 2007)
  - **Labour**: raise to 18 the age to which school must be in EE&T; create skills academies; literacy and arithmetic tests for school leavers.
  - **Conservative**: more power to head teachers; councils to be given control of education budgets.
  - **Liberal Democrat**: new schools. Extra teachers; reduce class sizes; one hour physical activity per child per day.
  - **SNP**: abolish graduate endowment and pay off graduate debt; cut class size to 18 in P1-P3.

- Taxation
  (Westminster 2005)
  - **Labour**: reform the "unsustainable" council tax; spending plans affordable without tax rises; tax relief for "hard working families".
  - **Conservative**: no "Third Term" tax rises; £4bn to cut taxes including £1.3bn cut in council tax for pensioners; possible cuts to inheritance tax and stamp duty.
  - **Liberal Democrat**: replace council tax with a local income tax; new 50% tax rate on earnings over £100,000 a year; raise stamp duty threshold to £150,000 to help first-time buyers.

  (Holyrood 2007)
  - **Labour**: no above inflation Council Tax increases.
  - **Conservative**: retain Council Tax with 50% cut for all households where occupants over 65.
  - **Liberal Democrat**: abolish Council Tax and set Local Income Tax from 2009-2010 (average rate 3.5% to 3.75%.)
  - **SNP**: abolish Council Tax and set Local Income Tax nationwide at 3p (at basic and higher rates.)

Question A3. (continued)

- EU (Westminster 2007)
  - **Labour**: adoption of proposed EU constitution after referendum; join the single currency if five economic tests show it is in UK interests; UK should be at "heart" of Europe.
  - **Conservative**: opposed to EU constitution and would hold early vote; UK to get powers back over fishing; quit the social chapter; oppose adopting euro.
  - **Liberal Democrat**: Work towards the right conditions for joining the euro, then call referendum; pro EU constitution.
  - In 2004 Michael Howard complained that New Labour was stealing every Conservative policy within days of it being unveiled; now accused of stealing Conservative policies on inheritance and "non-dom" taxes and Lib. Dem policy of taxing air travel.
  - Heavy prison sentences originally Conservative Party Policy.
  - Both Conservative and Labour vying to be seen as the more competent administrators of a free market economy.
  - Conservative admission that there will be no tax reductions during any first term in office.
  - Issue of 'green taxation'.
  - Absence of real differences seen as a significant cause of fall in election turnout.
  - Other relevant points.

STUDY THEME 1D: ELECTORAL SYSTEMS, VOTING AND POLITICAL ATTITUDES

Question A4

"Pass" and better answers should feature developed, exemplified knowledge and understanding of:
- The influence of social class on voting behaviour
- The influence of other factors on voting behaviour

and
- Balanced comment on/analysis of the influence of social class on voting behaviour.

Answers may refer to:
- various measures of social class: Register General's Social Scale, Standard Occupational Classification. The National Socio-Economic Classification Standard and links to voting behaviour.
- party support across social class seems to have continued along traditional lines; support was highest for the Conservatives in the top AB class and for Labour in the lower cohorts.
- Conservatives retained the largest share of AB vote and C1 vote. Share of C2 and DE rose from 2001 to 2005.
- Labour had the largest share of C2 and DE vote (but both fell).
- the Liberal Democrats increased their share in each group between 2001 and 2005.

Question A4. (continued)

- Labour has made long-term gains in the AB and C1 voters.
- Conservative lead over Labour in the ABC's down from 35% between 1974 and 1992 to 5% or less in the 1997, 2001 and 2005 elections.
- importance attached by political parties/ psephologists to sub-groups within social classes: Mondeo Man/Worcester Woman/ School Gate Mums.
- class dealignment - evidence that the electorate less committed (more floating voters) than in the past.
- Labour and Conservatives have won elections because they have been able to attract the support of people outside their core groups. While social class remains a strong indicator of party loyalty, social-economic divisions are much more complex than they used to be.
- Conservatives gained support amongst DE voters between 1997 and 2005.
- Labour gained support amongst AB voters between 1997 and 2005.
- changing nature of class.
- extent to which parties have abandoned their traditional ideological positions.
- in Scotland, different parties are in competition in socially similar areas. The electorate is aware of this and hence people of similar social backgrounds vote for different parties in different constituencies.
- the Rational Choice Model includes factors such as current issues, party leaders, past performance.
- the nature of the election, its importance, the workings of the electoral system being used are also now taken into account.
- Liberal Democrats did especially well in constituencies where there was a particular reason why voters might be disenchanted with Labour; those with large numbers of Muslim voters and those with large student populations.
- the Labour Party vote fell on average by over 5% more in seats with a relatively large Muslim population than it did in those with little or no such population. The increase in the Liberal Democrat vote meanwhile was around 5 points in such seats.
- the Labour Party vote fell by around 3% more in constituencies with large numbers of students, to the apparent benefit of the Liberal Democrat Party.
- the Green Party's best share of the vote (4.5%) came in constituencies where over 30% adults have a degree.
- the BNP did best in constituencies with relatively low proportions of people with a degree, especially if the constituency had a relatively large number of Muslims.
- UKIP did best in constituencies with a relatively large number of older people and, in places with few voters with degrees.

Modern Studies Higher
Paper 1 – 2008 (cont.)

Question A4. (continued)

- Labour continues to be strong in its traditional heartlands in Scotland, Wales and the North of England. The Conservatives in the East and the South. Only in the South West did the Liberal Democrats secure 40% or more. In geographic terms, Scotland and Wales remain central to any Labour majority.
- no Conservative MPs in the big cities such as Birmingham, Manchester, Liverpool, Leeds, Sheffield and Glasgow.
- although gender appeared to have had little influence on party preference (34% of men and 38% women voted Labour) - 34/32 for Conservatives - there was a lower swing to the Conservatives among women (1.5%) than among men (5%).
- research claims that turnout increases by 4% in constituencies contested by women.
- among those in the 18-34 age group, 38% voted Labour, 27% Liberal Democrat and 21% Conservative.
- evidence suggests that it is no longer the case that people become significantly more inclined to vote, as they grow older.
- more than 81% of successful candidates served in the previous Parliament and only 18% elected for the first time.
- other relevant points.

SECTION B - Social Issues in the United Kingdom

STUDY THEME 2: WEALTH AND HEALTH INEQUALITIES IN THE UNITED KINGDOM

Question B5

"Pass" and better answers should feature developed, exemplified knowledge and understanding of:
- Government policies to reduce gender and ethnic inequalities
- The impact of government policies on gender and ethnic inequalities

and
- Balanced comment on/analysis of the effectiveness of government policies to reduce inequalities.

Answers may refer to:
- Child Tax Credit and Working Tax Credit.
- Government sees affordable child care as crucial to narrowing the wage gap.
- Minimum Wage and Statutory Pay Obligations.
- Maternity and Paternity leave.
- since 2003 companies have had to give serious consideration to employees (both genders) with children under six who request flexible working hours: one in five working women and one in ten men have taken up this 'right to request'.
- Skills Strategy (July 2003) to address the fact that over 50% of women in part time work are working below their skill level.

Question B5. (continued)

- 2004: government set new Public Services Agreement targets for under-represented groups in senior management (two of which relate to women) for 2008.
- Equality Act (2006).
- Women's Enterprise Task Force.
- Work and Families Act (2006) extended the right to request flexible working.
- Gender Equality Duty Code of Practice (from April 2007) places legal responsibility on public authorities to demonstrate that they treat men and women fairly. (Implications for delivery of health care to both genders.)
- Public Service Agreement Targets:
  - 37% women in the Senior Civil Service (SCS);
  - 30% women in top management posts (Pay Bands 2&3);
  - 4% ethnic minority staff in the SCS;
- the Commission for Equality and Human Rights (2007).
- Race Relations (Amendment) Act, 2000.
- Ethnic Minority Employment Task Force (2004) to tackle unemployment among black and Asian people.
- Education and Training policies.
- One Scotland.
- strategic review of local race equality work in Scotland (2004).
- gender pay gap between 2005 and 2006 at its lowest value since records began.
- women now make up 60% of the university population.
- success of women in reaching senior posts varies from place to place. Glass ceiling only cracked, not broken.
- women make up 46% of all millionaires and are expected to own 60% of the UK's wealth by 2010.
- EOC research shows women make up less than 10% of the senior judiciary, senior police officers, top business leaders, national newspaper editors and 0.8% of senior ranks in the armed forces, despite accounting for over half of the UK population and 46% of the labour force.
- higher women rise up the pay ladder, the greater pay gap becomes; 23% at director level.
- gender pay gap: UK women in full time work earn 17% less per hour than men. (New laws urgently needed to tackle this according to EOC recommendation, September 2007.)
- pay gap higher in the private sector than in the public sector.
- 155% increase in equal pay cases being lodged with tribunals between 2006-2007.
- occupational segregation: 70% of women with qualifications in science, engineering and technology do not work in those professions.
- state pension not 'gender proofed'.
- 'wraparound' state childcare policy, from 8am to 6pm unlikely to be in place before 2010.

Question B5. (continued)

- women from Black Caribbean, Pakistani and Bangladeshi groups (despite 'stellar' GSCE performance), likely to face a higher risk of unemployment, lower pay and fewer prospects for promotion.
- the CRE says that local government and the criminal justice system (including the police) have made good progress. However Whitehall departments, NHS trusts, further education colleges, district council and the Olympic Delivery Authority have fallen short.
- whereas there are 3,460 white members of the senior civil service, only 70 are Asian and 20 black. Overall, just 4.1% of the top ranks come from a black or minority ethnic background.
- a study by the Joseph Rowntree Foundation, reveals that ethnic minorities suffer twice the level of poverty of white Britons, as discrimination and disadvantage blight their life chances.
- the study finds that many Pakistanis and Bangladeshis are paid so little they are still classed as poor. 'Income poverty' traps 1 in 9 whites, but 6 out of 10 Bangladeshis, 4 out of 10 Pakistanis and 3 out of 10 Britons of black African heritage.
- "We have helped an additional quarter of a million people from ethnic minorities move into work over the last few years and the employment rate has risen to 60% in the last three years. But we are aware that more needs to be done." (Jim Murphy former minister for employment and welfare reform).
- other relevant points.

Question B6

"Pass" and better answers should feature developed, exemplified knowledge and understanding of:
- the *collectivist* and *individualist* approaches to health care and welfare provision
- Government health and welfare provision policies

and
- Balanced comment on/analysis of the view that government, not individuals, should be responsible for health care and welfare provision.

Answers may refer to:
- Collectivist emphasis on responsibility of government to invest in health and welfare to counteract inequalities borne by those who are victims of an exploitive system.
- original Beveridge principles of the welfare state; funded by social insurance and taxation, with citizens being provided for 'from cradle to grave', specifically with regards to health, housing, employment, education and poverty.
- public health care should be funded from taxation.
- Individualist emphasis on a reduced role for government, 'lifestyle choices' and greater individual responsibility.
- view that there is no such thing as society, only individuals.

Question B6. (continued)

- individuals should provide for their own health care through the private sector.
- view that the collectivist approach encourages a 'dependency culture'.
- affordability of the welfare state dependent on getting even more people off benefit and into work.
- link between unemployment among lone parents and child poverty.
- Labour's 'Third Way' - the welfare state exists for those in genuine need, but individuals have to be encouraged to become more self-sufficient.
- promotion of 'social inclusion' through 'welfare to work' policies with private sector involvement.
- welfare provision governed by 'rights and responsibilities'/'a hand up, not a hand out'.
- targeting and means - testing of benefits.
- Government response to the Turner Report on pensions.
- proposals for benefit reform.
- NHS continues to be supported from taxation; with mainstream clinical services staying public but the advantages of private sector involvement to meet targets is welcomed (less so in Scotland when Labour administered).
- emphasis on 'healthy lifestyles'.
- Labour's 'holistic' approach to health and welfare: health is not seen in isolation - its relationship to social class is acknowledged.
- Government has achieved success in lowering unemployment but there are still concerns about the high number of, for example, IB claimants.
- the numbers in absolute poverty have gone down, but relative poverty has increased as the income gap between rich and poor has widened.
- health inequalities still a cause for concern.
- other relevant points.

SECTION C - International Issues

STUDY THEME 3A: THE REPUBLIC OF SOUTH AFRICA

Question C7

"Pass" and better answers should feature developed, exemplified knowledge and understanding of:
- The main aims and features of Black Economic Empowerment
- The impact of Black Economic Empowerment on reducing inequalities

and
- Balanced comment on/analysis of the effectiveness of BEE in reducing economic inequalities.

Answers may refer to:
- BEE originally seen as a broad-based government strategy that would transfer economic power to Blacks without disrupting the SA economy.
- BEE applies to skill, education and know-how as well as business.

Modern Studies Higher
Paper 1 – 2008 (cont.)

Question C7. (continued)

- 1998 Employment Equity Act aimed at ensuring black South Africans get preferential treatment in hiring, promotion, university admission and the awarding of government contracts.
- 2004 BEE legislation contained more rigorous affirmative action.
- BEE Codes of Good Practice 2007 (to be reviewed in 10 years), involve transferring ownership to black people and women, ensuring representation at board and management level and preferential procurement of goods and services from black-and female-owned enterprises: setting of ambitious targets within 10-15 years.
- introduction of "generic score cards" 55 of the 100 points focussed on workers and those unlikely to have a shareholding in the company.
- many of BEE's voluntarily agreed targets are modest and not all are expected to be achieved.
- BEE Advisory Council advises on and reviews BEE with aims of identifying sectors/stakeholders in economy that are BEE compliant.
- BEE mandatory only for government and state-owned companies but BEE credentials pretty much required for those wishing to do business with the state.
- less than 2% of companies (accounting for 61% of the GDP) have to wrestle with the full codes. Foreign companies exempted from some of the rules.
- first informal phase of BEE saw it appointing party loyalists to senior posts in state corporations and using them as training grounds for future capitalists and managers.
- in 2004 - 68% BEE deals went to 6 black-owned (top ANC members') businesses.
- growing and diversifying black middle class. BUPPIES (black and up and coming professionals) comprise 2.6 million "black diamonds" - a 30% increase in less than two years.
- Anglo-American appointed its first black CEO in 2005.
- Patrice Motsepe - first black South African to make it to the Forbes Billionaires List (2008).
- 7% of the Stock Exchange ownership has moved into black hands (target 25%).
- whites control 90% of the assets and big companies.
- most companies nowhere near target of 40% black managers.
- many black businesses have failed or are struggling but successful black-owned businesses are now part of everyday life.
- pace of BEE varies from region to region. Progress slower in Kwa Zulu-Natal than in other areas.
- many BEE deals said to collapse into cronyism and corruption.

Question C7. (continued)

- except for a minority of instant millionaires, the majority of black people remain on the edges of the economy.
- income differentials between blacks and whites have declined.
- number of wealthy black households has increased far more quickly than whites.
- low income black households have dropped but whites have risen.
- whites total income share has fallen but blacks has risen.

BUT

- increase in number of people in shanty towns (5 toilets between 7000 people in Foreman Road).
- only 5% blacks obtaining university entrance qualifications.
- as high as 77% of children in the best state performing schools are white.
- Among the unemployed, 52% of blacks have no access to a regular wage earner.
- half of the local authority areas do not provide sanitation, clean water or rubbish collection to more than 40% of their households.
- 2m families live in shacks with no running water.
- whites have higher proportion of skilled or very skilled employment.
- skills deficit very much in evidence - South Africa had to import 2000 workers from Taiwan to build a new SASOL plant.
- 4.5m unemployed and an additional 3.5m who have given up looking for a job.
- 80% of unemployed aged between 15-34.
- 4m living on less than $1 a day (2m in 1994).
- two thirds of South Africa's income held by a (mostly white) top 20%.
- view that BEE is about the transfer, not the transformation of power. It has turned South African into a 'cappuccino' society: a lot of black coffee at the bottom, a layer of white foam on top and a sprinkling of cocoa on the very top for show. There has neither led to a wider distribution of wealth nor to a greater opening up of opportunities for previously disadvantaged individuals.
- view that BEE is disempowerment for whites and Asians.
- other relevant points.

STUDY THEME 3B: THE PEOPLE'S REPUBLIC OF CHINA

Question C8

"Pass" and better answers should feature developed, exemplified knowledge and understanding of:
- Evidence of 'democracy' in China.
- The 'undemocratic' features of Chinese society.
and
- Balanced comment on/analysis of the extent to which China is becoming a more democratic society.

Answers may refer to:
- constitution guarantees the fundamental rights of all citizens, including freedom of speech.

Question C8. (continued)

- in March 1999, the National People's Congress (NPC) included the concept of rule of law into China's constitution.
- more open reporting of issues of concern in the media.
- political reform officially on the CPC agenda and is being introduced from the bottom up.
- contested elections in villages every three years since 1988, but these are controlled by the CPC through the selection/monitoring of candidates; direct elections at village and more recently township level are by law supposed to be free but local officials are thought to interfere/manipulate; evidence of arrests of villagers/lawyers who protest about selection process/results.
- talk of elections at county level and perhaps higher.
- Hong Kong (since 1997): half of government is non-communist and democratically elected although the leader is appointee of the CPC; free press, freedom of association, etc.
- 2007 saw first ever contest in the election (chosen by committee of 800 pro-Beijing 'voters') for the chief executive of Hong Kong - winner had to put on a show of electioneering.
- reform of the legal system in response to the market economy.
- in 2006 the Supreme Court reclaimed the power to review all death sentences.
- dissidents allowed to funeral service of deposed party chief Zhao Ziyang in 2005 and in November 2006 CPC organised a public commemoration of the 90th anniversary of the late Hu Yaoang, ousted because of reformist beliefs.
- widening of CPC membership to private business people who make up one third of membership but this is seen more as a pragmatic move to support business and not to extend democracy.
- anonymous text message on mobile phones prompted inhabitants of Xiamen to join one of the biggest middle class protests of recent years (May 2007). Protest (successful) was against plans to build huge chemical factory on a site in the suburbs.
- China remains a one party state with the Communist Party of China (CPC) in overall control.
- CPC controls the government by screening appointments and promotions to all posts: all appointments must be approved by the level above; there are elections to local and national congresses but direct election only at the lowest level.
- Organised opposition to CPC banned.
- CPC's power not as great as in earlier years; weakened by fiscal and administrative decentralisation but CPC continues to control the overall direction of policy.

Question C8. (continued)

- report on Building of Political Democracy in China 2005 stressed the continued rule of the CPC. 'Democracy' in CPC speak does not mean allowing organised opposition.
- CPC does not allow free speech, a free media or organised protests but more grassroots organisations/activities beginning to develop; CPC tries to manage those who threaten indirectly and suppress those who challenge directly.
- Reporters Without Borders (RSF) rates China 163/167 in the world for press freedom.
- outspoken newspapers or editors sacked. *Bing Dian* closed in 2006 reputedly as part of a long-nurtured scheme to silence the paper's "pursuit of democracy, rule of law, deliberation, liberty and rights", according to its editor.
- high number of imprisoned journalists - 31 in 2006.
- Police force of 30,000 on-line monitors - dissidents who net-post views are imprisoned.
- evidence of lengthy detentions without trial for dissidents.
- no open elections in Hong Kong before 2017 and all candidates will have to be approved by central government. 2020 at earliest before Hong Kong citizens will have the right to directly elect all members of the city's legislature.
- crackdown on Falun Gong.
- events in Xinjiang and Tibet.
- other relevant points.

STUDY THEME 3C: THE UNITED STATES OF AMERICA

Question C9

"Pass" and better answers should feature developed, exemplified knowledge and understanding of:
- The powers of the President of the United States of America
- The ways in which Congress and the Supreme Court can check the powers of the President

and
- Balanced comment on/analysis of the effectiveness of Congress and the Supreme Court in checking the powers of the President.

Answers may refer to:
- powers of the President laid out in the Constitution.
- Chief ambassador - determines foreign policy and diplomacy; appoints ambassadors and diplomats.
- may propose legislation at any time; calling a press conference; making an announcement at a public event.
- can issue rules/regulations and instructions (Executive Orders)* that have the force of law and do not need Congressional approval *but may be declared unconstitutional by the Supreme Court.* (*173 in Bush's first term).
- submits the budget to Congress.
- signs legislation; can refuse to release money for legislation that he disapproves.

Modern Studies Higher
Paper 1 – 2008 (cont.)

Question C9. (continued)

- President can issue 'signing statements' in which he gives directions about the ways in which legislation should be understood and interpreted.
- can adjourn/recall Congress *but Congress does not have to pass any laws during special sessions.*
- may veto legislation. Must act within ten congressional working days of receiving a bill from Congress. Only vetoes bills he is likely to be unsuccessfully challenged on (always studies final passage votes). In 2001-5, Bush was the first president since 1841 to get through an entire 4-year term without using a veto.
- Bush's first use of the veto was in July 2006 (Stem Cell Research Enhancement Act). *A two-thirds majority vote in both the Senate and the House can override a veto as was the case in November 2007 (a bill authorising spending on water projects) - the first successful overturning of a presidential veto since 1998.*
- for a brief period between 1997 and 1998 Clinton had the 'line item veto' power *until the Supreme Court declared it unconstitutional.*
- 'pocket' veto can be used only at the end of a congressional session. *Congress cannot override.*
- runs the executive branch of the federal government and nominates executive branch officials and all federal judges (including the 9 Supreme Court Judges). *Senate confirms appointments by simply majority vote.*
- may make a 'recess appointment'. Bush's recess appointment of John Bolton as US ambassador to the UN bypassed the need for Senate confirmation.
- acts as Commander in Chief of armed forces (has power to wage war while constitutionally Congress declares and funds it); may call out the National Guard.
- In 2002 Bush claimed an inherent presidential authority to order military actions to pre-empt hostile action against the USA. What constitutes a threat is at the discretion of the president.
- Negotiates treaties. *Congress scrutinises and a 2/3 Senate majority is required for ratification.*
- *in 2007 Bush lost the power to negotiate trade deals without Congressional backing.*
- may commute a sentence (commuted Lewis 'Scooter' Libby's 30 month prison sentence in 2007) and issue a pardon at any time, even before a crime is charged, *but the power to grant pardon does not extend to impeachment.*
- appoints the Executive Office of the President.
- may make 'personal interventions' and issue 'statements'. When a Bill banning the 'cruel, inhuman and degrading treatment of detainees by Americans anywhere in the world' was signed, a statement was issued reserving the right of the President to flout it.

Question C9. (continued)

- the House of Representatives may impeach the President. Senate conducts the trial. *(Speaker Pelosi has made it clear that impeachment proceedings against either the Vice-President or the President are "off the table").*
- Legislative and nominee filibusters.
- Supreme Court can declare the actions of any member of the executive branch, including the President, to be unconstitutional. (Judicial Review).
- when the Supreme Court ruled that Mr Bush had exceeded his authority in setting up, without congressional approval, special military commissions to try some of the Guantanamo detainees, the President pushed through the 2006 Military Commission Act giving him just such authority.
- 'Terri' Schiavo case (2005).
- resignation of US attorney general Alberto Gonzales seen as a congressional 'scalp'.
- President often referred to as 'bargainer-in-chief'.
- No Child Left Behind legislation passed with bipartisan support because the Democrats liked the extra money Bush threw in to sweeten the deal.
- Bush's reform plans for social security failed - as did those on immigration (but was able to end 'catch and release' via an address to the nation).
- Bush found it difficult to get bills through Congress (before Democratic 2006 mid-term elections successes) because of divisions in his own party.
- presidential power traditionally thrives in emergency and crisis conditions.
- claim that Bush has marginalised Congress and established an 'imperial presidency'.
- second term Presidents seen as 'lame ducks'.
- other relevant points.

STUDY THEME 3D: THE EUROPEAN UNION

Question C10

"Pass" and better answers should feature developed, exemplified knowledge and understanding of:
- The positive consequences of enlargement
- Concerns over recent and possible future enlargement

and
- Balanced comment on/analysis of the impact of enlargement on the EU.

Answers may refer to:
- increase from 15 to 25 members in 2004, to 27 in 2007.
- Romania and Bulgaria became the 26th and 27th members at start of 2007.
- Croatia is engaged in formal membership talks. Macedonia has achieved candidate status and others are waiting in the wings.

Question C10. (continued)

- the Copenhagen criteria for membership include democracy, a free market economy, observance of human and minority rights, and political stability.
- stronger, peaceful and more stable Europe - lead up to membership has stimulated a wide range of social and economic reforms in new member states.
- has further promoted the rule of law and respect for human rights in new democracies.
- has helped the east European countries as they moved from communist central planning to liberal democracy.
- a more influential voice in international affairs.
- countries of western Balkans have been pacified and stabilised after the bloody 1990's thanks mainly to their hopes of EU membership.
- weakens Franco-German domination.
- opportunities for business.
- cheap labour good for economies of richer members.
- UK, Ireland and Swedish economies said to have gained the most. (They immediately fully opened their labour markets to workers from the new entrants.)
- closer cooperation in dealing with crime.
- changes made in Turkey to boost hopes of membership.
- French and Dutch rejections of the constitution in 2005 partly reflected dissatisfaction over the 2004 enlargement.
- fears that EU machinery, originally designed for 6 members, cannot function effectively with 30 or more members.
- the *widening* (admitting new members) as against *deepening* (further integration of new members) dispute.
- impact on decision-making procedures - each member has veto on foreign policy making.
- relocation of business to countries with lower labour costs and worse social protection.
- immigration control issues.
- implications of extension of Schengen Agreement, which allows people to cross borders without having their passports checked, to 25 members (not UK and Ireland).
- demands on structural funds; losers and winners in development aid stakes.
- budgetary issues - UK rebate; CAP reform (or lack of it).
- new members likely to resist initiatives that cost more than they can easily afford.
- concerns about some new members being too pro-USA and too quick to provoke Russia.
- Poland the only member to block the start of negotiations with Russia on a new partnership agreement.
- Polish threat to veto any alteration to voting rights.
- many measures judged necessary to ensure that the enlarged union could continue to function put on hold by EU constitution stalling in 2005 after referendum defeats in France and Holland.

Question C10. (continued)

- Nice Treaty can only function in a union of a maximum 27 members - no more can join until a new treaty is in place.
- UK and Denmark now joined by Poland, Hungary and the Czech Republic as non-euro members.
- Turkey accepted as eligible in 1963. If it ever joins it could become the most populous member by 2020 with more voting weight and more MEPs than Germany.
- David Milliband's suggestion that the EU should expand beyond Europe to Russia, Middle East and Africa.
- implications of the Lisbon Treaty.
- enlargement brings economic benefits, cements political stability in Eastern Europe and lessens the prospects of a federal Europe.
- other relevant points.

STUDY THEME 3E: THE POLITICS OF DEVELOPMENT IN AFRICA

Question C11

"Pass" and better answers should feature developed, exemplified knowledge and understanding with reference to specific African countries (excluding the Republic of South Africa) of:
- The role of education and health care in development
- Other factors that contribute to development

and
- Balanced comment on/analysis of the importance of education and health care to successful development.

Answers may refer to:
- education and health care provision (neither widely available free of charge in Africa), seen as fundamental to a country's economic and social development.
- impact of literacy levels, school enrolment, levels of expenditure on health and education (public and private) in both actual and percentage terms, life expectancy, and infant/child mortality rates on development.
- lack of properly trained teachers, overcrowded classrooms, lack of teaching resources.
- African countries cannot afford to fund free health care. Health care professionals attracted by conditions in more developed nations.
- impact of HIV/AIDS and malaria.
- initiatives to eradicate extreme poverty and hunger/empower women/make cash available to encourage local businesses (on average it takes 64 days to register a business in Africa).
- importance of property rights and the rule of law.
- impact of other factors on development: good governance, conflict, debt, aid (and its uses), international investment, globalisation, types and levels of a country's natural resources.

Modern Studies Higher
Paper 1 – 2008 (cont.)

Question C11. (continued)

- Millennium Project has set up 12 "research villages" (target of 1000 by 2009) in 10 African countries to pioneer models of development (The Magnificent Seven) that can be copied but there is an admission that successful implementation depends upon foreign aid.
- even when aid is "properly" used, development does not come overnight: when Zambia's foreign debt was reduced; most of the savings were spent on recruiting teachers and improving health care (fees for basic health care removed). Nevertheless, Zambia remains poor and still depends on aid.
- Mali is one of only five African countries to have fully qualified for America's Millennium Challenge Account with its stringent criteria for good governance.
- Niger is the second poorest country on the planet but it is a democracy and has a free press. There has been a very slow response to its problems.
- according to the IMF, Africa's economy is growing steadily but this masks differences between countries whose economies are improving (in many cases those rich in natural resources) and those, like Zimbabwe, and more recently, Kenya, whose are going backwards.
- similarly, there are development differences within specific countries. (Sudan has an oil-rich but undeveloped south complementing an educated, commercial north with few natural resources). Northern government feels no obligation either to share its wealth with poorer peripheral provinces or to behave well towards them.
- recognition by **both** the UN Investing in Development: A Practical Plan to achieve the Millennium Goals **and** the Commission For Africa that "more aid is needed to meet Africa's development needs". However "outsiders cannot deliver development, it must be done by Africans" (Commission for Africa report).
- Africa's population continues to increase with nothing like the required rate of economic growth to sustain it. Population growth has been described as the 'unmentionable', the elephant in the corner of the room.
- other relevant points.

STUDY THEME 3F: GLOBAL SECURITY

Question C12

"Pass" and better answers should feature developed, exemplified knowledge and understanding of:
- The part played by the USA in achieving global security
- Concerns about the part played by the USA in achieving global security

and
- Balanced comment on/analysis of the part played by the USA in achieving global security.

Question C12. (continued)

Answers may refer to:
- significance of both UN and NATO membership.
- spends the most money on UN peacekeeping. Pays about 26% of the cost for UN peacekeeping missions - size of contribution limited by US domestic law.
- has frequently led demands for reform of the UN, hinting that otherwise its financial contribution may fail.
- support crucial to election of Ban Ki Moon as UN Secretary General. View that the USA supported a weak candidate in order to undermine an organisation with which it has always had problems.
- provides 0·5% of UN peacekeeping personnel - president retains command of military personnel.
- view that without strong US leadership and involvement the UN would not amount to much and there is no hope of a peaceful and stable future for humanity this century.
- gives protection to NATO and strongly supports the NATO Response Force.
- preferred to act alone after 9/11 despite NATO invoking Article 5 of its treaty - an attack on one ally is an attack on all.
- chose allied units in coalitions of the willing to go to war (on terror) in Afghanistan.
- protracted US/NATO difficulties in Afghanistan, where Americans bear the brunt of the fighting.
- invasion of Iraq in 2003, led by USA and UK (opposed by France and Germany): consequences for long-term peace and security in the area.
- NATO as a whole declined to send troops to Iraq (apart from a small training mission) but eventually agreed to take over ISAF (International Security Assistance Force) in Afghanistan.
- Taliban and Saddam Hussein speedily toppled from power but war on terror has since appeared to go less well.
- US forces retain responsibility for hunting down al-Qaeda's fugitive figurehead Osama Bin Laden.
- relentless US diplomatic pressure to secure peace in the Middle East (Road Map); pressure on Israel to withdraw from Lebanon.
- USA-led Proliferation Security Initiative as a response to concerns over spread of WMD.
- 2007 Creation of AFRICOM (U.S Africa Command).
- USA played a big role in ending the war between north and south Sudan but the UN's failure to stop either the atrocities in Darfur or the nuclear posturing of Iran and North Korea has stemmed largely from the inability of the so-called P5 (of which the USA is one) to agree on what should be done.
- USA opposed the Ethiopian invasion of Somalia in 2006 to topple the Union of Islamic Courts but gave assistance after the event.
- October 2007 sanctions against Iran seen as a reflection of USA's despair at the UN.

Question C12. (continued)

- Russia blames US push for eastward expansion of NATO and US support for groups that have toppled governments in the former Soviet sphere of influence for increased tension.
- plans for USA's missile defence plans for Europe seen as a threat to global security by Russia - USA accused of reigniting the arms race. Russia has threatened to place missiles in Belarus and has halted its participation in the Conventional Forces in Europe Treaty.
- US policy towards North Korea and Iran (axis of evil), has heightened tension but could be seen to reduce nuclear proliferation and through joint diplomacy with others, has secured agreement for North Korea/Iran not to develop weapons-grade nuclear material.
- USA (has positioned the 2nd aircraft carrier group in the Gulf) seen as being on a collision course with Iran which it accuses of support for insurgents in Iraq and over Iran's continued attempts to develop regional supremacy.
- USA rejected the International Landmine Treaty.
- USA has given immunity to US subjects involved in actions to combat terrorism.
- accusations that the USA is a major arms supplier worldwide.
- Americans emphasise counter-terrorism and counter-insurgency, Europeans are more comfortable with peacekeeping and stabilisation.
- USA is in a position to play a decisive role in achieving global security - given its military, economic and technological capabilities - but it has always had a tendency towards unilateralism.
- other relevant points.

Modern Studies Higher
Paper 2 - 2008

1. Daphne Millar claims: "*The most common reasons for not handing in a prescription are to do with cost [or the price per item is such that many adults find it very difficult to pay] - no-one finds that they did not need it after all.*"

   Source C1(a) shows that 28% of people didn't hand in prescriptions because it cost less to buy the medicine over the counter, while 25% didn't hand it in because it cost too much money. However 10% of people said that their health improved - did not need it after all.

2. (a) Daphne Millar claims: "*Free prescriptions would make a huge difference as to whether patients did or did not go to their doctor.*"

      Source C1(b) show just over 10% would be much more likely to go/it would make no difference to almost 80%.

   (b) Tom Beattie claims: "*In a recent survey on health care systems in European countries, the UK was one of the highest rated.*"

      Source C2 shows that 7 out of the 11 countries had their health care systems rated/scored higher than the UK.

3. Tom Beattie claims: "*Most people who have to can afford to pay for all the items on their prescriptions and that there is little support from health and community groups for completely abolishing prescription charges.*"

   Source C1(c) shows that more than 60% can afford all of the items but Source C3 shows 50% support for abolishing prescription charges.

4. Credit will be given for:
   A style appropriate to a report (sub-headings, chapters etc) with:
   - an introduction that indicates an awareness of the role to be adopted and makes a clear recommendation
   - developed arguments in support of the recommendation
   - identification of and comment on (rebuttal of) counter arguments
   - synthesis of source information
   - provision and use of appropriate background knowledge
   - an overall conclusion.

   Arguments for the proposal may feature:
   - charges may lead to suffering and poorer health
   - experience in Wales
   - effects of cost especially on lower income groups
   - long term damage to health when prescriptions not taken up
   - evidence from GPs
   - costs relative to overall NHS budget
   - impracticality of lump sum payments

Modern Studies Higher
Paper 2 - 2008 (cont.)

Question 4. (continued)

Arguments against the proposal may feature:
- spiralling cost of drugs
- exemptions already protect the poor/children/elderly
- option of buying over the counter
- charges discourage time wasters coming to surgeries
- adverse effect on the provision of new drugs
- benefits will be for the better off not the poor
- will lead to cutbacks elsewhere that will worsen the health gap

Your answer may also include background knowledge-based argument developed from references in:
- Source A
  - The Scottish Government... ... ... phase out and eventually abolish... charges
  - the effects on individuals and in the longer term on the NHS
  - the founding principles of the NHS
  - an immediate improvement in the health of the nation
- Source B
  - the rising costs of medicines
  - the NHS has... enjoyed public support
  - the financing and performance of the NHS in Scotland
  - If the health gap is to be closed

Other background knowledge may include:
- the extent and causes of ill health
- the extent of poverty
- foreign comparisons
- recent media coverage
- relevant personal experiences
- other relevant points